# The Radical Community of Faith

A Vision for Its Structure, Agenda and Objectives

A Study Guide to the Epistle of Ephesians

**Beryl Forrester**

Partnership Publications

Partnership Publications
www.h2hp.com

# The Radical Community of Faith

A Vision for its Structure, Agenda and Objectives

by Beryl Forrester

© 2015 by Beryl Forrester

Published by
Partnership Publications
A Division of House Publications
11 Toll Gate Road, Lititz, PA, USA
Tele: 717.627.1996

www.h2hp.com

All rights reserved.

ISBN-10: 0996292411
ISBN-13: 978-0-9962924-1-2

Unless otherwise noted, scripture quotations in this publication are taken from the *The Holy Bible, English Standard Version® (ESV®), copyright © 2001 by Crossway, a publishing ministry of Good News Publishers. Used by permission. All rights reserved.*

Printed in the United States of America

## Dedication

This is a study guide to the book of Ephesians. While written nearly two millennia ago, Ephesians is particularly consistent in addressing issues facing the Christian community in West Africa. Here some commentary is provided on a portion of a chapter and includes ideas to help the reader discover how the text is inviting us to change, to grow and to become more Christlike.

I dedicate this writing to my many brothers and sisters in West Africa who are hungry for growth in their personal faith and are searching for the radical way of being a community of Jesus' disciples as understood in the early centuries: the 325 years before Constantinianism became the model for being Christian and doing church.

# Contents

Introduction ................................................................ 7

Overview Notes ......................................................... 14

Lessons

1. Spiritual Blessings in Christ ........................................... 22
2. Radical Disciples of the Exalted Christ ........................... 33
3. But God! Rich in Mercy ................................................ 45
4. Walls Broken Down and a Temple Built ....................... 61
5. The Revelation of God's Mystery of the Ages ............... 77
6. Finding Spiritual Strength ............................................. 96
7. A Community Worthy of Christ .................................. 106
8. Two Men: One Old; One New
   Two Paths: One to Death; One to Life ....................... 124
9. Indicators of New Life in Christ ................................. 139
10. The Household Codes ................................................ 156
11. The Challenge to Divine Warfare ............................... 169

Appendix A: Constantinianism's Impact on
Church History; the Anabaptist Alternative ..................... 186

Appendix B: An Overview of Anabaptist Hermeneutics .... 193

Appendix C: Figures 1-5 ................................................... 199

Appendix D: Book of Ephesians ....................................... 214

## Introduction

*So then you are no longer strangers and aliens,*
*but you are fellow citizens with the saints*
*and members of the household of God,*
*built on the foundation of the apostles and prophets,*
*Christ Jesus himself being the cornerstone,*
*in whom the whole structure, being joined together,*
*grows into a holy temple in the Lord.*
*In him you also are being built together*
*into a dwelling place for God by the Spirit.*

Ephesians 2:19-22

These lines from Paul in Ephesians 2 give us the Bible's most succinct definition of the community of disciples—the Church—as it was formed by Jesus 2000 years ago. The purpose of this study guide is to help West African believers to do church as defined in these verses.

It is imperative for the followers of Jesus in any age, to check how they are doing and experiencing church against the foundation of the first century apostles and prophets as they understood Jesus Christ, the church's cornerstone.

The New Testament writers of the Gospels, the Epistles, Acts and Revelation were men who had first-hand experience with Jesus: They heard him teach, saw his miracles, watched his interaction with those to whom he ministered as well as with his critics. They were there when he was crucified and they saw the resurrected, glorified Christ. They were with the throng upon whom the Holy Spirit was poured out at Pentecost. The New Testament writers give us the clearest and most authentic picture we can have for Christ's vision of his community. That is why this study guide is of utmost importance to the church in West Africa. It is a vehicle to take us back to the beginnings of the community of believers founded by Christ and his apostles and prophets. With that target, and with Holy Spirit guidance, we will be equipped to do church and be church the way Christ envisions it for his followers in all ages and cultures, including here in West Africa.

The study guide attempts to contextualize the gospel—that is, we want the good news to be read and understood as the Word spoken directly into West African culture. In using the West African designation, I in no way wish to single out this geographic area for either good or ill. It means simply that God's message of salvation applies just as much to us here as to people in North America, Europe or any other place on God's good earth. God is calling people everywhere to re-creation and transformation into the model of his Son, our Savior Jesus Christ.

This way of knowing and following Jesus is known as radical Christianity. The term radical in current English usage has been corrupted into conveying the idea of something like the lunatic fringe of a cult. However, radical, in its best sense, simply means going back to the roots. (*Radix* is the Latin for roots.) The New Testament, Matthew through Revelation, is our portrayal of the first-century roots of the Christian faith as understood, envisioned and practiced by the first generations of Jesus' followers. This is our foundation, and it is to that foundation that we must return time and time again as we seek to be faithful to the Lord of the church, Messiah Jesus.

The most helpful preparation you can do as you pick up this study guide is to, at least temporarily, set aside religious, intellectual and cultural biases and traditions and come with an open mind to listen to what our cornerstone, Messiah Jesus (along with the apostles and New Testament prophets) wants us to know about being the faithful community of Christ. Keep in mind that the end product is not just more knowledge but a deeper commitment of faithfulness to being Christlike. For Paul the objective is that "we all, with unveiled face, beholding the glory of the Lord, are being transformed into the same image [of Christ] from one degree of glory to another. For this comes from the Lord who is the Spirit" (2 Cor. 3:18).

Although the study guide can be used individually in personal Bible study, there is a significant advantage to doing the study in small groups of believers seeking community faithfulness where we can together listen to what the Spirit is teaching us.

This study guide is presented in collaboration with Christian Health Education as biblical and theological background to CHE strategy training. CHE is based upon a wholistic and radical understanding of Messiah Jesus. The CHE philosophy is that people are a wholistic creation and that the Good News of Jesus addresses all aspects of God's creation needing healing and transformation into the Lord's design for His creation. CHE practitioners and trainers must be well versed in this foundational understanding of the Gospel as it informs biblically based community development.

## Additional tips on using the Study Guide

The chapters of Ephesians roughly divide themselves into two lessons per chapter. As you study, always have your Bible open to the text for that particular lesson. Read the biblical text several times.

Biblical references appear as Rev. 3:7-10, Rom. 6:1-2 and so forth. A reference without a book title means the passage (such as 2:3-4) is in Ephesians.

## If you have questions

If you have questions, email the author at berylforrester@gmail.com. He is particularly interested in reading your answers to the questions at the end of each lesson.

## The Radical Community of Faith:
## A Vision for Structure, Agenda and Objectives

1. We are a Christlike community dedicated to reflecting Jesus' character, spirit, life, teachings, relationships, servanthood and dedication to the will of the Father. Jesus Christ is the acknowledged head of the community and it is our purpose, both individually and collectively to be growing up into our head.

2. We are built on the foundation of the apostles and prophets, Christ Jesus himself being the cornerstone. We regard the first century community of Jesus and his apostles as an authoritative model for the faith and life of the church through the ages, made real within our own cultural context. The things that happened to God's people prior to the advent of Christ must be viewed through the ethic and teachings of Jesus. We must challenge our own traditions and cultures and evaluate them in light of Christ and the apostolic witnesses.

3. We are a community of peacemakers, showing consideration, mercy, pardon and love towards everyone, even our enemies. We know that peacemakers are in opposition to the divisive, destructive tactics of the enemy and we are prepared to suffer in the proclamation of the gospel of peace and righteousness.

4. We are in submission to our head, Jesus Christ and to each other as we are filled and empowered by the Holy Spirit. We give and receive counsel within the brotherhood, enabling us to be in oneness with Christ and each other.

5. It is of primary importance for us to be fully engaged with God's mission of salvation; bringing and doing his will on

earth as it is in heaven and making known "the mystery of his will, according to his purpose, which he set forth in Christ as a plan for the fullness of time, to unite all things in him [Christ], things in heaven and things on earth" (1:9).

6. We are a community of worship, declaring the righteousness and sovereignty of Christ both in our gathered times and by our daily conduct as we move among the general society.

7. We have a high sense of responsibility for each other. We share with those among us who have material needs, we mentor and admonish each other in our walk with Christ, we suffer with those who are suffering and celebrate with those who rejoice and celebrate.

8. The leaders among us are those who emerge with gifts of caring for the flock and equipping the saints for the work of ministry. Leaders may be appointed and credentialed, but they are in no way elevated above anyone else in the community. Leaders are first and foremost servants, not masters. The source of authority in the community is the gathered believers, who together discern the will of the Lord and provide direction for the community.

9. The church is a welcoming, inclusive community, accepting among us persons at whatever faith level they are as they come. We welcome people who are open to the transforming power of Christ, teachable and ready to find identity among us. We are a community of pardon, forgiveness, mercy and patience. Condemnation and judgment may be in order on rare occasions, but grace and hope freely abound among us.

10. Persons who publically declare their intention to become disciples of Jesus and who demonstrate in their conduct that they are dying to sin and are being resurrected to newness of life in Christ are invited to become members of the fellowship through the symbol of water baptism.

11. We believe God's salvation is for all people; therefore, we understand the community of faith as a place where former walls, divisions, hostilities and prejudices have been eradicated by the reconciling death and resurrection of Christ. We regard ourselves first of all as citizens together in God's kingdom.

12. We are a people of eschatological hope. In our life together under the Lordship of Christ we are already realizing the fruits of the eternal reign of Christ wherein we are set free from the powers that mar and destroy God's good creation. At the same time we live with the limitations of human mortality and falleness with our eyes of faith fixed on the future culmination of God's victory over Satan where all evil, mortality and the enemies of God will be judged and forever and eternally banished.

## Overview Notes
### Major Themes of Ephesians

God, in the generosity and infinitude of his grace, has blessed all people regardless of ethnic background. He has chosen and invited them to be his new people, adopted them as his own sons and daughters and opened to them the great mystery of his plan for time and eternity: that through Christ he is gathering up and transforming all of his creation, and most importantly all people, into a divinely intimate, eternal union with himself (1:10; 3:9-10).

Of utmost importance to us in this plan of gathering all things under Christ is the critical role of the church in bearing witness against the powers that are defeated. How do we know they are defeated? Look at the lives of Jesus' followers and see how satanic powers have lost control over those who are faithful to Christ.

In Ephesians much emphasis is put on the Christian's responsibility to walk in the light and shine the light of Christ, exposing the darkness. There is a consistent call to living in obedience to Christ so that the brightness of the light is not compromised.

Readers are encouraged to lay hold of the wisdom to understand the power that enabled Christ to live as an ordinary man, a life of total faithfulness to the Father's will. This wisdom and power raised and exalted Christ above all the powers of the cosmos. This very power now enables the community of believers to live a life that reflects God's righteousness for the whole world to see (1:18-23). People, at one time dead in sin, have now been raised to life eternal in Christ and are seated with him in the heavenly places far outside the control of the evil ruler and empowered to do good works (2:10). Examples of some of those good works are enlarged on in Ephesians chapters 4-6.

Christ is celebrated as the one who brings peace and togetherness (2:11-22). Those who at one time were strangers, outcasts and enemies are welcomed to share in the new family of God, his holy temple. Together we are the new chosen people authentically recreated into the image of God and by his grace we maintain our covenant with him. This was accomplished through the self-giving act of Christ's death and resurrection that dealt the death blow to cosmic evil powers.

The first three chapters of Ephesians are an extended praise to God for what he has done through Jesus Christ for the church. Chapters 4-6 address the response believers are expected and enabled to embody as benefactors of God's grace; how to act in response to the re-creation they enjoy as God's people. The second half of the epistle notes the good works, which God prepared beforehand, that we should walk in them (2:10).

## Understanding Paul

In Ephesians Paul presents a somewhat broader understanding of his themes compared to his other epistles. Although these divergent views could be read as contradictions, they are better understood as a more mature Paul, perhaps making some adjustments in his developing theology and as a way of making the epistle relevant to numerous circles of churches (including us in West Africa 2000 years later).

It is of interest to enumerate these themes as a way of gathering a more holistic vision of God's power and grace in our lives and communities. When Paul says *church* in some of his writings, he refers to a gathering of believers in a specific location. In Ephesians, the term however, has taken on a more universal connotation: a family of communities of Christ scattered over a broad expanse of geography. In some instances Paul conveys that end-time salvation is something that will be occurring in the near future. (Rom. 13:11, 1Thess.1:10; 4:13-5:11). In Ephesians, however, believers are already made alive together with Christ and raised up with him and seated with him in the heavenly places (2:4-8). He depicts our present position in Christ, even now, as a resurrection life. Our new life in Christ is an actual down payment on what is to come. Some refer to this as the now and not yet quality of being in Christ. Ephesians mentions nothing of a second-coming, future appearance of Christ.

In Ephesians nothing is said of salvation in relation to justification, of being made righteous through the faithfulness of Messiah Jesus. Instead, salvation is simply a benevolent act of God's grace (2:5-8).

In some cases Paul portrays Christ himself as engaged in battle with the evil powers; in 1 Cor. 15:24, it is Christ who does battle destroying every rule and every authority and power. But in Ephesians 6:10-18, it is the well-armed believers who engage the battle with the powers.

## Words to Note

### Faith/Faithful

*(Gk. Pistos)* In the Pauline epistles, English translations usually render this term as have faith in or believe in or believe on. Preachers and teachers explain it in a way that conveys faith essentially as "intellectual assent or acceptance of a given fact or assumption." In our enlightenment, we are expected, especially in our minds, to agree with the teaching being presented; for example, Jesus was born of a virgin, he died on the cross to take away our sins, and he is coming again.

While these are all true and valid biblical beliefs, it is doubtful this is what the apostle Paul was attempting to communicate in his words that are translated as faith or believe. Such a narrow understanding of faith/belief probably contributes significantly to contemporary shallowness of Christianity and the absence of fruitfulness in the lives of many believers. The Hebrew understanding of faith goes far beyond getting one's intellectual synapses lined up behind a propositional statement. The biblical meaning of faith is to be trustworthy in one's faithful obedience to a covenanted relationship with God. For examples, see Eph. 6:21; Matt. 25:21; 1 Cor. 4:2; 2 Cor. 1:18; 3 John 1:5. The phrase "believing in Christ" is better translated as acting faithfully in and through Christ.

In Ephesians the term *in Christ* appears more than 20 times. Being in Christ can mean nothing less than total and utter faithfulness to his will for us. It is all about a relationship and connectedness with Christ. Our actions (good works) are modeled and empowered because of our full identification with, and participation in, what God is doing to recreate his world to the righteous perfection it once had.

## Subordination, submission and headship

These words require careful examination in the context of Ephesians; otherwise, African men, who already have cultural value of male superiority over women, are provided with further "scriptural" grist to maintain the status quo of servile, unquestioning obedience on the part of women towards their husbands.

The instructions to the wives (which are surprisingly brief compared to what is expected of the husband) are in 5:22-24 and half of v. 33. Her subordination is parallel to her subordination to Christ and to the church's subordination to Christ. Her relationship to her husband is brought into sharper focus as it corresponds to her relationship to the Lord and Savior, Jesus Christ. Throughout Paul's writings the marriage relationship is a metaphor for the relationship of Christ with his body, the church. The relationship of Christ to the church is utterly faithful and self-giving. The church is voluntarily subordinate to Christ as head out of love and respect for the way he has given himself and for the mission he is yet engaged in. The same rationale must be part of the husband-wife relationship.

In scripture the English words *subordination* and *head*, from the Greek *kephale*, can have two significantly different meanings. In Ephesians 1:10 Christ's headship refers to his supremacy and authority over all of God's creation. In Ephesians 5, head refers to source or goal into which we grow as we mature in Christ.

This second understanding is clearly implied in the instructions to the husband (9 verses). He is to provide his wife with the loving, caring and nurturing resources that will enable and encourage her to grow up into Christ. He is the resource she needs to fulfill her ministry to the family, the church and the broader community. As African husbands get a better handle on their responsibilities as leaders in the home, as nurturers and liberators of their wives, we are going to see some astonishing growth in the church.

## Salvation; to save

In popular usage today, salvation often means being able to go to heaven when I die. Others understand the gospel to be primarily a set of beliefs which must be accepted as truth. Acts 16:31 says, "Believe in the Lord Jesus, and you will be saved." For some, believing certain things about Jesus (that he was born of a virgin, that he died on the cross for the forgiveness of our sins and that one day he will return) guarantees salvation. All these are correct; however, it is best if we look at a more complete usage of salvation in the New Testament.

For the Jews of Jesus' day, salvation meant that God would raise up a new king for them, one even more glorious and powerful than David. This king would drive the pagan Roman overlords out of their country, and Israel would once again be a mighty force among the nations of the earth.

Some Jewish people, like Simeon (Luke 2:29-32) and the Apostle Paul, understood salvation as the extension of God's saving grace far beyond the Jewish people to include all people regardless of ethnic background. In Jesus, God was establishing a new chosen people who would live as a glorious testimony to the righteousness and love of God.

Jesus also made frequent use of the term salvation. For example, Zacchaeus was a Jew, but because he collaborated with the Romans and became very rich, his fellow Jews considered him outside the possibility of redemption. But once Zacchaeus repented of his greed, restored money he had stolen and changed his relationship with others, Jesus pronounced him "saved."

The rich young man who wanted to be assured of salvation and eternal life, felt it necessary to see what Jesus would recommend for him in this regard. Jesus knew this man intimately and could see that what stood between him and eternal life were his riches. So Jesus challenged him to divest himself of his wealth and distribute it to the poor, then come and be a disciple of Jesus. Jesus' follow-up comments offer little hope for this man's salvation.

From Jesus and other New Testament writers, it is evident that the meaning of salvation cannot be easily squeezed into simple either/or categories. Salvation is both something which we do, and at the same time, something done on our behalf out of the grace and mercy of God.

It should be apparent that the New Testament has no simple definition for salvation. Saved from the power and consequences of sin? Of course. From alienation from God and our fellowmen? Yes, indeed. From the fear of death? Certainly. From illness? Perhaps. From poverty? Sometimes.

Salvation will vary with each of us according to our own needs and how God desires to recreate us into the likeness of Christ.

Discipleship is neither a way of earning salvation nor a fruit of salvation. Discipleship is living as a follower of Jesus through the power of the Holy Spirit. That is the experience of salvation in the here and now, with our eyes fixed on the ultimate experience of salvation in God's eternal kingdom when this life is over.

# Lesson ONE

## Spiritual Blessings in Christ
Ephesians 1:1-14

### Lesson 1 Passage overview

The first two verses of greeting are typical of Paul's letters. He wants it understood that he is an apostle (messenger) of Jesus, by the will of God. The receivers are the holy ones in the region of Ephesus, a thin slice of land connecting Europe and Asia. He connects them with the grace and peace of the Father God and the Lord Jesus Christ.

The letter opens with a two-way blessing. The believers are blessed through the redemption, forgiveness of sin, salvation and inheritance of sons of God. They are chosen to live to the praise of God's glory; thus God blesses himself by having a people who are recreated in his image, living a life that is a credit to his holiness.

But not only are the adopted sons saved, God's salvation extends throughout the cosmos to the entirety of his creation, all of which is even now being gathered up under the authority of Jesus Christ. These are words of sublime worship and euphoria, so great is the glory, power, beauty and love of God's blessing upon his creation.

God's blessing is guaranteed by the Holy Spirit, and his holy people are specifically recreated in Christ to worship God above all, through their holy living.

***Blessed be the God and Father of our Lord Jesus Christ*** tells us that blessing, honor and worship belong first to God, for he is the one who stands before all things, all time, all creation and all persons. In saying this we claim him to be the head of all things including Jesus Christ. He is the great heavenly Father who cares for, nurtures and sustains all that is.

We should specially note that as Father of Jesus Christ, it is through Christ that the Father exercises authority over creation. We also conclude from this statement that the nature and character of God are known to us through Jesus Christ. Jesus shares the title Lord because it is through him that the saving presence and activity of God become available to us.

***Who has blessed us in Christ with every spiritual blessing in the heavenly places*** implies that future blessings of being in God's presence are already, in real life, experienced by those in the community of Christ. The language in these verses is deliberately excessive and repetitive to celebrate his immeasurable love towards us. These ecstatic words of gratitude speak forcefully of the Father's benevolence.

## The spiritual blessings in Christ (1:4-13):

These blessings include being *chosen* and *predestined* even before creation, by God's initiative, to be his adopted sons, in and through Christ. Use of the masculine offspring term carries a suggestion of royal status and should be understood as comprising both men and women. We are predestined for the purpose of doing the part he has designated and gifted us to fulfill in his eternal plan of making all things new. We join him as sons who have serious responsibilities of bringing glory, honor and praise to him, our Father.

We are being holy and blameless as we live and rest in his loving presence. Holiness and without blame are characteristics of lives as we respond to his grace and experience his transforming blessings towards us. His blessing makes us capable of offering him a holy and blameless life. If we are not willing to live in a holy, blameless manner, a mirror reflection of Jesus, Son of Man, we have no reason to think or pretend we are Christian.

Paul, and indeed the Bible throughout, intertwine worship and ethics. The Bible allows no separation between what we usually think of as formal Sunday morning worship and our behavior the rest of the week. Holiness and blamelessness is a 24/7 proposition. We render worship to God as much through routine actions as we do through our formal services by gathering in a special building on a specific day. We are enabled to live for his glory both now and through eternity.

We are redeemed (bought out of slavery to sin and Satan) by the blood of Christ. His blood recalls the Passover sign on the door posts in Goshen by which God's people were spared the death sentence and set free to become his special community.

We are set free from the guilt and penalty of our sins because of his abundant grace that he lavished unsparingly upon us. In verse 7 there is no suggestion that the blood of Christ was required to appease an angry deity. Rather, Christ willingly gives up his life out of God's treasury of grace to redeem a people to himself once and for all. The phrase *wisdom* and *insight* refers both to lavished grace now and to God's eternal plan.

We are brought into the loop of *knowledge* (wisdom and insight) about God's plan for cosmic restoration. From the beginning it has been his plan to gather up all things in heaven and on earth in Christ. God's ordering of events in time and eternity has been and continues to be administered (managed) by Christ. The gathering up is more than an end-time event; the plan has been in process from the beginning, through the Old Testament period, the advent, life, death and resurrection of Messiah Jesus, on through the church and on into God's future climaxing when the time for gathering in and gathering up will have been fulfilled. Rather than viewing time as a succession of elaborate dispensational watertight eras, there is a steady, certain revelation of the fulfillment of God's plan since creation. We are called first and foremost to covenant faithfulness, even if we do not understand how all this gathering up happens. Christians fully trust and worship the one who is sovereign over past, present and future.

The Spirit is the *guaranteeing inheritance* we receive from our Father. The Holy Spirit is the assurance that God is always with us as we participate with him in the messianic work of reconciling all things to him. The Spirit assures us that what God has already done belongs to his eternal plan and what he says he will do in the future is likewise firm. Although we have not yet received all the promised blessings, we are, without equivocation, sealed into the eternal scheme of what God will do. If we presently experience walking in the Holy Spirit, life itself is an act of worship; the work of the Holy Spirit in our life today is the guarantee of what is to come in the future. For both present and future we live to the praise of God's glory. For the Christian, all of life is our worship to the praise of God's glory.

**Open our hearts**

Pray-read Ephesians 1: 3-14

Gracious Father,

I am overwhelmed at your love and power, at the blessings of heaven that you have lavished upon us, your adopted sons and daughters. I know that your love has been with us even before the creation of the world, and it was there even when mankind, the highest of your creation on earth, rebelled against you and tried living without you. Thank you that your love bridged the gap and that you were willing to send your beloved son Jesus into the world to rescue and redeem us from the enemy. I thank you, from the depth of my heart and soul, that you are so eager to receive us back into your family and that you did not just barely let us squeak in, but you have lavished onto us every spiritual blessing that is found in the heavenly places. I thank you that Jesus came to bring us your word, hope and life. I thank you that in him we understand everything we need to know about you in this life.

I praise you for anointing Jesus to give his life for us as the Passover lamb who broke the power of the enemy in and among us forever. I thank you for removing the guilt of my sin and setting the account clear between yourself and each one of us.

Thank you for the gift of the comforter who is among us and within us, creating us into the image of Christ and empowering us to live a truly holy life, free from the power and stain of sin. I want to live that holy, blameless life because that is how the world around us will know who you are and will desire to join us as part of your people.

I thank you for bringing us into the circle of your plan for making all things in heaven and on earth new. I willingly and joyfully give you my life for you to use to bring your kingdom and your will here on the earth. I want to experience in every way possible your kingdom come. Thank you so much for the inheritance of wisdom, life, righteousness, peace and joy you have already poured out upon us, and this is only a token of what is to come!

Thank you for the many faithful servants who shared the word of truth and the gospel of salvation making it possible for me to come into this relationship with you.

Please, in your grace, continue to make me into the image of Christ. Open my eyes and my heart to the ways you yet want to refine and disciple me. I have but one goal and desire, which is to become more and more like Jesus. To the praise of your glory. Amen.

## Transform our lives

Imagine your life as a house with several rooms. Each room represents a significant part of your being: your family and friendship relations, how you use the material things necessary for life, your occupation/career, your heritage and traditions, your sexuality, your recreation, leisure time, and similar rooms.

Take a walk through the first room on the left accompanied by your friend—the Holy Spirit. You perceive the room is already occupied by a spirit presence of the resurrected Christ who is playing with the children, chatting with your wife, greeting the neighbors, phoning your brother-in-law—in short, doing all the things you enjoy doing with your friends and family.

Each room has a small adjoining closet with a door firmly closed and locked. Only you have the key to the closet door, and you are aware of each item in that room; each one is inventoried, boxed and carefully resting on the shelf. The Holy Spirit encourages you to open the closet door as well; you concede.

He hands you a box from the bottom shelf and asks you to open it. It's a box full of bad memories of hurts from your childhood, times when your older siblings belittled and shamed you because you could not perform as well as they did. Those memories still hurt and they have built walls between you and your siblings. The memories also dominate many of your relationships, creating walls of mistrust and suspicion.

You place the open package back in its place on the shelf. The Spirit hands you another box, this one from the top shelf. You slowly open it, knowing full well its contents. It's a box of intricate, odd shaped contrivances: your personality problems. There are several contraptions in this one: the way you attempt to dominate others into serving your personal goals, the anger you often feel welling up inside when others excel, your assumed superiority because of your ethnic background and your determination to always be socially upwardly mobile.

There are several more boxes in this closet. You don't need to open each one; you are all too aware of every item inside each box. As you become uncomfortable in this small space with the Holy Spirit, you start making moves as if you wish to leave.

But as you do that, a series of phrases from Ephesians 1:3-14 start flashing across the screen of your mind:

- blessing in the heavenly places
- chosen us in him before the foundation, holy and blameless before him
- adopted as sons
- blessed in the beloved
- forgiveness of our trespasses
- the riches of his grace

Your feet are glued to the closet floor. The Spirit puts a supporting arm around your shoulder as your body falters under the realization of the inconsistency between the Ephesians phrases and the contents of this closet. The Spirit holds you close and says, "Come, I'll help you carry these out back to the compost heap."

As you and the Spirit wrestle the ponderous boxes outside, he keeps playing over and over these words of Jesus: "If anyone's will is to do God's will, he will know. . . . "

"With us," he reminds you, "there's no line between knowing and doing. With Jesus, if your will is to do the Father's will, you obey him and you will do his will."

As you make the final trip from the closet to the backyard, you check the calendar and you realize much time has passed, nearly a year, in the process of clearing out the closet. Spiritual and behavioral transformation, if it's for real, is typically a long, slow process. But finally, the boxes with their contents are on the compost heap, and already the worms are busy transforming them into ordinary garden soil, forever obliterated.

Gradually you see family and friends in a new light. Relationships with each other are better. The barriers, walls and loops of razor wire are gone. There are more smiles, welcomes and hugs. Even our characters are included in God's transforming plan for the fullness of time, to unite all things in him, things in heaven and things on earth.

## Christology

An important way to read a passage of scripture is to ask questions: What do these verses tell us about Jesus Christ? How does this passage inform us about the man who came as Word to reconcile us to God, bringing us into His family? What do these verses say about the mission, the work, the person of Jesus Christ from eternity past, his advent, life, teachings, death, resurrection, as bridegroom of the church and the one who gathers up all things for eternity?

Reading Ephesians 1:1-11, look carefully at all the phrases that inform our Christology:

1. He calls some to be his apostles (sent ones)
2. He is the one to whom we are faithful
3. He is our source of grace and peace
4. His Father is the Lord God Jehovah, the great I AM
5. He opens to us access to all the spiritual blessings that are in heaven

6. We have been chosen to be in him since before creation. He causes us to be holy and without blame before the Father
7. He made it possible for us to be adopted as sons of God
8. It is through him we receive the glorious grace of God
9. His violent, self-giving death has bought us out of slavery to sin and Satan
10. His grace cancels the guilt of our sins
11. Through him God is bringing to pass his will for time and eternity

Ask any West African how he perceives the mission of Jesus Christ and most will tell you, "Jesus came to die on the cross to take away my sins so I can go to heaven when I die." They give that answer because they have been taught by pastors and missionaries who have a low or minimal view of Christology. This investigation provides us with clues as to why Christianity in many countries seems so shallow on a personal level and so ineffective in creating truly Christian community.

This view comes from centuries of both Catholic and Protestant theology that attempts to deal with the overwhelming sense of guilt about sin because most believers lack discipleship and faithfulness to a covenant relationship with God. God, in much of Catholic and Protestant theology, is understood as a distant, angry and capricious Deity, as our pagan ancestors thought of him centuries ago.

This Christology trivializes the love, power, grace and transcendent majesty of the perfect Son of Man. It is a me-focused theology that attempts to appease, manipulate and gain favor with the deity as did the ancient pagans. The book of Ephesians invites us to return to the apostolic, radical (back to the roots) understanding of Christ, the Messiah Jesus who invites us to become God's faithful, new covenant people.

## Reflection, Discussion, Action

1. A foundational theme of Ephesians is found in 1:9-10 [God's] "purpose, which he set forth in Christ as a plan for the fullness of time, to unite all things in him, things in heaven and things on earth." In about 25 words explain the importance of the verse. What is God's plan for the fullness of time? How does it affect you?

2. This phrase is from 1:4: "that we should be holy and blameless before him." List at least six aspects of your behavior that illustrate your holiness and blamelessness.

3. List the six spiritual blessings in the heavenly places which Christ blesses us with. Memorize this list and be prepared to explain why each is important and how it has changed your life.

4. What do we mean by a full Christology as compared to a limited Christology? What difference will a full Christology make in the way we experience life in Christ?

# Lesson TWO

## Radical Disciples of the Exalted Christ
Ephesians 1:15-23

### Lesson 2 Passage overview

The verses are a repeat of the blessings of the previous verses except that they are cast in the form of an intercessory prayer on the part of the apostle. With his readers' glorious position as adopted sons of God, Paul prays that they will receive wisdom, understanding and knowledge of Jesus Christ equal to their exalted status in Christ. He pleads for enlightened hearts to connect to the hope of their calling to the same mighty power that raised Christ from the dead.

Again he repeats the status of the exalted head, Christ: at the right hand of God, above all power and authorities now and throughout eternity. The body of Christ is none other than the church, the community of the faithful growing up and into the head.

Verses 15-23 are similar to verses 3-14, which in the original Greek text is a single, rambling sentence. In this one, Paul begins with a thanks/blessing, then moves into an intercessory prayer reciting God's initiatives towards the readers and how the believers come to know and join in with his blessings. Verses

20-23 provide an elaborate summary of the mission, work and exaltation of Messiah Jesus together with God's eternal plan for creation and cosmos.

## "Your faith in the Lord Jesus and your love toward all the saints"

Paul begins this section with a strong pastoral affirmation of the believers—he has been made aware of their faithfulness to the Lord Jesus and their love towards each other. The thought could likewise be stated in the inverse: their love for Jesus and their faithfulness to one another in the body of Christ. This is Paul's starting point and he is headed towards tying his blessed readers to the triumphant fulfillment of the plan of God for time and eternity.

What a lift it is for Christians to hear this kind of affirmation from someone who has an apostolic and pastoral relationship with them! Paul blesses the believers with warm words of God's grace and power. There are probably plenty of reasons why he could have spoken otherwise to them, but he chooses to bless and affirm them. Paul knows that the way to facilitate forward movement spiritually and relationally among Christians is to bless and encourage them. Visioning, affirming words have great motivational and cleansing power in our lives and relationships.

Can you imagine how exciting our Sunday morning preaching, praise and worship services would be if we were served up great heaps of blessing and affirmations as we gather together following a week of trudging through the difficulties of life's ups and mostly downs? When Christians are blessed, affirmed and encouraged they leave the service prepared and empowered to face the challenges for the next six days and the future beyond.

When I first arrived in West Africa and was adapting into my role as a missionary, I attended an evangelical, Pentecostal mission church. Sunday after Sunday the preachers, selecting mostly graceless Old Testament texts, beat the congregation with rods of iron: "You unfaithful, backsliding pawns of Satan, he is about to make you fall and set your feet on the broad way to hell. You can't hide your sinfulness from God." On and on, the preacher chastised the congregation for more than an hour.

I soon learned this is normal fare for most West African church services (I hesitate to refer to them as worship services.) It appears most African pastors believe they haven't done their Sunday morning duty unless they've gone on with a seemingly endless rant of threats, scoldings, warnings and intimidations. Both Jesus and Paul used words of woe and warning when they were called for, but in the usual setting where a pastoral leader meets with Jesus seekers, the words need to be comforting, caring, challenging, nurturing, healing, affirming and visionary.

And why not? Look at the present and future we have ahead of us: God has raised Christ from the dead and seated him at his right hand in the heavenly places, far above all rule and authority and power and dominion, and above every name that is named, not only in this age but also in the one to come. And he put all things under his feet and gave him as head over all things for the church (1:20-22).

That is the message Paul has for his flock and it is the same message West African Christians need to be hearing regularly from their pastors and teachers.

Instead of focusing on the exalted Christ, the head of the church who is seated at the right hand of God above all rule and authority and power and dominion calling us to become his presence in our communities, West African believers are too often encouraged to understand Christ as a power source to be manipulated for personal benefits such as these:

- deliverance from curses
- a big house, an elegant car and a beautiful wife
- a visa to America
- healing for my aching back
- frustrating the devil's plans against me
- getting an appointment to a government post
- motherhood for a barren woman
- (worst of all) enjoying the benefits of being a Christian and at the same time indulging in the pleasures the flesh and all the world has to offer.

Church, as experienced by many West Africans, is mostly about ourselves and our exaltation, how can I have honor, prestige, power and position and material wealth. What many African believers hear from the pulpit on Sunday is simply a reflection of the heart of the preacher, who has a prosperous, flesh-oriented vision for himself. Many West African churches have little more than a window dressing of Christianity, thinly disguising traditional animistic religion complete with shaman (the pastor), ritual incantations and sacred paraphernalia all coming together to engage in deity manipulation. All for a price, of course (tithes and offerings).

The question really is how can we be delivered from where we are now to be where God wants us, his adopted sons and daughters, seated with Christ among the spiritual blessings of the heavenlies and working together with him gathering up all things into Christ?

We start by praying and laying ourselves before our loving heavenly Father. (See the "Open our hearts" pray-read section below.)

A question surfaces in our minds as we read Eph. 1: 20-21. We are told that the mighty working of God defeated the power of Satan when he raised [Christ] from the dead and seated him at his right hand in the heavenly places, far above all rule and authority and power and dominion, and above every name that is named, not only in this age but also in the one to come. The list of powers, potencies, and forces is so complete it leaves nothing in this age or in the one to come outside the rule of Christ.

If indeed Christ is elevated to a position superior to all powers, good and evil, in this age, why are the evil powers still uncontrollably doing their worst in our world? Why, in chapter 6:10-20, are we given such detailed instructions of battling the enemy if he has been rendered powerless? We could add here the reference from Col. 2:15: "He disarmed the rulers and authorities and put them to open shame, by triumphing over them in [Christ]."

A helpful perspective is to say that what God has accomplished in Christ has been done to empower the church in this evil age to finish what needs yet to be done—putting the evil powers to open shame through the exaltation of Christ. His purpose is that through the church the manifold wisdom of God might now be made known to the rulers and authorities in the heavenly places" (Eph. 3:10).

Although the war has been won, the evil powers remain unconvinced. The church has the task of demonstrating that evil is defeated in the daily lives of those who follow Jesus. Our presence in this evil world puts us in the unique position of informing and overcoming the powers. The task of overcoming them is done through the immeasurable power of God available to us as sons of God. That same power that raised Christ from the dead is also at our disposition as we carry on the battle against evil.

God's renewing of his creation and salvation is still in full swing. The transformation God envisions for his creation is an on-going, long-term process. The followers of Christ in this world are fully engaged in the on-going conflict and struggle. But we don't lose heart because of the antichrist, which you heard was coming,—is in the world already. "Little children, you are from God and have overcome them, for he who is in you is greater than he who is in the world" (1 John 4:3-4). Also, reassuring words to Joshua as he was preparing to do battle against Ai: "And the Lord said to Joshua, "Do not fear and do not be dismayed. Take all the fighting men with you, and arise, go up to Ai. See, I have given into your hand the king of Ai, and his people, his city, and his land" (Joshua 8:1).

Even before the battle, God has already given the enemy into our hands! Christ in us is immeasurably greater than the evil powers in the world around us with whom we do battle.

Probably the greatest challenge is that many Christians in West Africa haven't decided yet whose side they are on in this battle. Far too many Christians would like an imaginary foothold on both sides. The enemies of Christ appeal to us with offers of power, prestige and material prosperity. Jesus offers a cross, inviting us to join him in his earthly journey as a suffering servant in a messy battle to do God's will on earth as it is in heaven. We can't have it both ways; either we take up the cross and follow our Master or we join the worldly powers.

Many, even among those preaching on a Sunday morning, have yet to decide whose camp they are in, to be faithful as Messiah Jesus was during his life on earth, or caving in to the appeal of the enemy.

## Open our hearts

Pray-read Ephesians 1:15-23

*We need to be praying for ourselves and the West Africa church* as Paul prayed for the Ephesians:

*We pray for a spirit of wisdom and of revelation in the knowledge of God.* We need to be filled with God's wisdom about spiritual realities, and we need him to increase our knowledge of his plan and design for time and eternity. We need enlightened hearts so that our heart is the same as God's heart of re-creation for ourselves and the entire cosmos.

*We need to take our eyes and hearts off worldly, material things and pray to know the hope to which we are called* and what are the riches of his glorious inheritance to us, the saints

(1:18). Our inheritance from God has nothing to do with material wealth and personal pride. It has everything to do with being in an abiding, loving relationship with God and his people.

*We pray for the immeasurable greatness of God's power toward us* who are faithful and ask God to work the same great might he worked in Christ when he raised Christ from the dead and seated Christ at his right hand in the heavenly places (1:19-20). We will never arrive at those heavenly places in our lives and churches until we go through the death and resurrection experience with Christ. It is only as we die to ourselves and our fleshly desires that God's power is able to effect resurrection life in our lives and churches.

*We pray for contrition and willing submission to Christ,* the head over all things for the church (1:22). We covenant to be in communion with Christ that we may be filled with all the fullness of God. We pray, we ourselves will be gathered up into Christ even as we are joined with him in his mission of gathering up all things and putting all things under his feet.

## Transform our lives

Here we have ten statements that represent radical Christian discipleship. Read through them carefully and thoughtfully. Do these statements describe where you are or where you would like to be in your faith development and your commitment to following Jesus? If some are new to you, are you interested in exploring them further? Are there habits, worldviews or sins that need to be changed on your journey to becoming a radical follower of Jesus?

1. **The teachings and example of Jesus are the norm for believers.** Jesus is understood as our model; we live by the rule of Christ (John 13:12-20; 14:53-58; 1 Pet. 1:14-15).

2. **We are here as servants, not masters.** Through servanthood we demonstrate the transforming power of Christ. We suffer with others as a means of bringing them the healing and salvation of Christ. God's kingdom is advanced through the power of suffering love as opposed to power tactics of the flesh (Heb. 2:9-10; 1 Pet. 2:12, 20-24).

3. **Through a non-coercive proclamation of the good news we invite others to voluntarily follow Jesus.** Through servanthood and example we call attention to God's presence and mercy already in their experience. We help others build their faith upon ways they already see and know about God. We meet people at their current faith level with terms they are able to comprehend (1 Cor. 2:1-5).

4. **The Old Testament is read and understood through the lens of Jesus-ethic.** The New Testament is authoritative in the life and faith of the church. The Bible is discerned and interpreted among the gathered believers under the leading of the Holy Spirit.

5. **We are active peacemakers.** We resolve conflicts of our own and for others through mediation. We seek to end cycles of violence by returning good for evil. War and all forms of violence against others are never an option for the Christian (Matt. 5:9; 23-25).

6. **We live in community with other believers.** We both give and receive counsel from the community. Preserving relationships in the community is of highest priority.

7. **Disciples of Jesus are those who are submitted to the Word are open to the counsel** of the church and eagerly continue their own transformation into Christlikeness.

8. **We believe Jesus has broken down all walls that would divide us**, such as gender, tribe, economic, ethnic, age and race.

9. **We live both in the now and the not yet.** The community of Christ daily demonstrates the earthly reality of life in God's kingdom. And we look forward to the completion of time when there will be a new heaven and new earth where Jesus Christ will reign supreme and all evil will be forever banished.

10. **We are ready to challenge the values and practices of our culture when they violate the Spirit and teachings of Jesus.** We don't allow the world to squeeze us into its mold when that mold diminishes Christlikeness in ourselves or others (Rom. 12:2).

## Christology

Ephesians 1:15-23 informs our understanding of the person and mission of Jesus Christ.

- He is the focus of our faithfulness.
- He was raised from the dead by the great might of his Father.
- He is enthroned at the right hand of the Father in the heavenly places.

- He is far above every rule, power, authority, dominion and name throughout eternity.
- All things are put under his feet.
- He is the head of all things for the church.
- The church is his body.
- His body, the church, is filled with the fullness of God.

Our list of Christological attributes keeps getting longer and longer. Please, let's not trivialize Jesus' unfathomable, eternal greatness by continually saying that his main reason for being was to die on the cross so we can go to heaven when we die. This diminished, minimal view of Christ is a root cause of shallowness in the West African church.

## Reflection, Discussion, Action

1. When you gather on Sunday morning with the saints, what personal, spiritual needs do you bring? What do you need in a worship service that encourages and empowers you to faithfulness in the coming days? What gifts and encouragements do you bring that might be a help and a blessing to others in the service? List the qualities of a sermon that edifies and encourages you in your walk of faith.

2. How do you respond to people who have questions about God's wisdom for allowing evil and hardship to be such a significant part of our existence here on earth? How do you help a doubter understand how God's purposes are being fulfilled and he is in the process of bringing all things under Christ?

3. Why are Africans attracted to the prosperity gospel? What is the appropriate course of action for a believer who finds himself in a church where what many African believers hear from the pulpit on Sunday is simply a reflection of the preacher's heart where Jesus is not allowed to reign?

4. As you read through the ten statements, which three do you feel most comfortable with? Which three do you find difficult and challenging? In what ways do you need to be moving your faith and experience so that they are based more firmly on the foundation of the apostles and prophets, with Christ himself the cornerstone?

# Lesson THREE

## But God! Rich in Mercy
### Ephesians 2:1-10

### Lesson 3 Passage overview

The first two words of this passage indicate that it is directly on the heels of the last verse in chapter 1: "And you" is in the plural indicating the entire church body, not individuals. Verses 1-3 list the qualities of a life under the control of Satan. Then comes the highly charged "BUT GOD" of verse 4. In contrast to those under Satan, you, the church, have been raised and seated with the exalted Christ in the heavenlies.

This is followed by two qualities of our salvation: it comes because of God's mercy and it is for the purpose of good works. Three vivid transformations contrast the before and after for those in Christ: we and you, death and life and sins versus good works. Salvation is understood as being liberated from the oppressive dominion of Satan. From this point on, the faithful are identified with Christ and his task of bringing everything under his authority.

Chapter 2 of Ephesians sees the world divided into two camps, two kingdoms, two cultures and two in several more ways of understanding being. This two-compartmented world is seen in sharp relief, one side as opposed to the other, one side for death, the other for life, one exhibit of the before, the other exhibit showing the after. It's a worldview not easy for us postmoderns to understand. We prefer a pluralistic, multi this and multi that world.

The apostle, however, invites us to set down those glasses and view the world as God sees it. Thus, while we may be comfortable with a multiplexed world, the ultimate God view is otherwise; and we do well to take heed and make the necessary adjustments to living in his reality.

The easy acceptance of a worldview other than what God is doing through Messiah Jesus has left West Africans scrambling to erect a façade Christianity, a false front disguising a convenient mix of traditional beliefs and flesh-pleasing options. The challenge here is to set all that aside and enter into covenant with the great I AM in which the community of Christ on earth is a flesh and blood portrayal of God's righteousness. This covenanted community plays a major role in the gathering up of all things into the exalted Christ.

*2:1-3 And you were dead in the trespasses and sins in which you once walked, following the course of this world, following the prince of the power of the air, the spirit that is now at work in the sons of disobedience among whom we all once lived in the passions of our flesh, carrying out the desires of the body and the mind, and were by nature children of wrath, like the rest of mankind.*

The first three verses of this section bluntly describe life under the control of the powers of evil. Here is a portrayal of life outside the kingdom of God characterized as an oxymoronic living death. The living dead walk—that is, conduct themselves in trespasses and sin, boldly disobeying the law of God. A son of disobedience is a person who lives contrary to the Creator's righteousness because he has an evil father whose orders he follows. Thus they are children of wrath destined to ultimately face a righteous God in judgment.

The fact that disobedience is noted tells us that there is a choice: a decision is made as to which power we will obey. Further, the text suggests that the natural, easy and alluring inclination is to live by the passions of our flesh and follow the crowd like the rest of mankind. If it appeals to the mind and body, that makes it ok. "Just do it!' as the Nike tag line proposes. We also take note that the sons of disobedience are following an overwhelming ruling spirit power dominating the very air we breathe. Mankind is enveloped by an evil spiritual power so strong and controlling of our volition we find ourselves locked into a rebellious living-death struggle against God.

At the end of this sorry state of affairs with damnation, wrath and punishment on the horizon, the drums roll and the trumpets blast: "BUT GOD." But God, being rich in mercy, because of the great love with which he loved us, even when we were dead in our trespasses, made us alive together with Christ (vv 4-5). The wealth of God's mercy and the magnitude of his love for mankind and all of his creation is the great show stopper of history. God's love, the very core of his being, impels him to reconciling intervention for the salvation of his creation.

The we and us of this sentence is the inclusive of community of those who have responded positively to God's offer of amazing grace. We at one time were dead in sin and among the enemies of God, but now are made alive together with the risen

Christ. Being raised together with Christ links God's intervention on behalf of his suffering, victimized Son with our own rescue. As his one and only beloved son is snatched (liberated) from the powers of death and destruction and raised, transformed from the body of dust to life eternal, we likewise and coterminously are adopted into divine sonship. We get a feeling for the magnitude of God's love and grace when we contemplate that the one act of intervention on behalf of his beloved, perfect son reached even down to us disobedient sons, children of wrath, rescuing us from the realm of death with the offer of divine sonship. Provided, of course, that we hear, respond and permit Him to make this liberating transformation in our lives. Understanding our redemption in relation to the resurrection of Christ enriches the meaning and significance of the term *in Christ* or *with Christ*.

With this "But God" amazing intervention freshly in mind we do well to fast forward to Eph. 3:10-11 where we find God's purpose in the transformed earthly existence of his liberated people, the church: so that through the church the manifold wisdom of God might now be made known to the rulers and authorities in the heavenly places. This was according to the eternal purpose that he has realized in Christ Jesus our Lord.

The only way the church can possibly make known the wisdom of God's might is if they (we) are radically changed from sons of disobedience to sons who look and act like the Father. When believers continue to live by the passions of their flesh, the evil rulers and authorities are not going to be convinced of anything, and we have betrayed God's power of resurrection. Only when our lives are transformed into Christlikeness are the evil powers truly shamed and shown as defeated. This is the great mission of the church.

*For by grace you have been saved through faith* is a slight variation from what is typically Paul. Usually he says that we are justified by faith in anticipation of future salvation.

Ephesians, however, does not mention justification and salvation as having already taken place. In Ephesians, being saved means liberation from the evil, oppressive rulers of the air. Having been liberated, the believer eagerly anticipates the day when all things will be subsumed under Christ.

This thought is immediately followed by *this is not your own doing; it is the gift of God, not a result of works, so that no one may boast.* Liberation from the evil powers comes not from our own noble efforts. In fact, we are so blinded and bound by sin that we are helpless to do the noble efforts. Liberation comes rather with the "But God" intervention of divine love and grace.

*For we are his workmanship, created in Christ Jesus for good works, which God prepared beforehand, that we should walk in them.*

Verse 10 tells of a second action on the part of God. First he liberates us from slavery to sin and second, he recreates us in a way that enables us to bring glory to Himself through our conduct, the way we live. His workmanship rewires us in such a way that the same way Jesus lived in the flesh now becomes our way of living in the flesh. The fruits and qualities of Jesus' life are abundantly and manifestly reproduced in us, his disciples.

The Greek for *workmanship* is *poiema* from which we have the English word *poem* or the French *poésie* provides a fascinating slant on how we understand workmanship. Not only has God recreated us as a smooth running mechanism, such as a top quality Swiss watch, he also created us with purposeful finesse and artistic appeal as in a poem.

## A theological sidetrack

This is an appropriate juncture for us to get off the mainline for a couple of miles to look at a collateral theological issue. *Faith*, in typical Protestant theology, refers to the trust we have that the salvation offered to us by God is a true, reliable proposition. Salvation, according to the Protestant template, happens when one intellectually and emotionally owns the proposition, repeats a sinner's prayer and accepts Jesus into his heart. Done. After that he is free to randomly dabble a bit in good works to show appreciation to God for his salvation.

But good works, still from the Protestant view, must be handled with discretion. If you do them too much or too vigorously people will soon get suspicious that you are attempting to earn your salvation. In Protestant thought, faith is often juxtaposed against works. Works are understood as righteous deeds done to secure divine favor, and woe to anyone who falls for that. Old Testament covenant law is viewed as an especially hopeless way of relating to God. Suspicions about good works are precisely the slightly open door Satan is looking for as entry to weasel his way back into one's life. This loophole, along with trivialized Christology believing that Jesus came just to die on the cross so

I can go to heaven when I die is a major venue to the shallowness of West African Christianity.

Radical Anabaptist thought understands the Greek *pistis* (faith), as encompassing the faithfulness of God and Messiah Jesus rather than the believer's faith in a proposition. Of course, we do need to be people of faith; confidence and trust in God are absolutely essential in our relationship with God.

Thus, as used here in v. 8, we could say that our salvation is grace (a gift) from God whom we know is fully trustworthy. We have that trust in him as God who unfailingly keeps covenant. God offers us his salvation because his Son, Messiah Jesus was totally faithful to the Father in his human experience encompassing his actions, teachings, example, death and resurrection. Because of his totality of faithfulness to his Father he has the title—Son of Man. He was the second and perfectly faithful Adam. Thus salvation is possible for us because of divine faithfulness.

Our salvation is activated as we respond by dying to self and being recreated in the image of the resurrected Christ in our relationships, our sexuality, our ethics, our creation care, the way we talk, how we use our resources—the list goes on and on. Therefore good works are not just an option; they are what we do and are 24/7 because the previous life bound by sin is dead, and the new has been created in Christ Jesus [expressly] for good works.

Good works are not a pre-requirement for salvation, nor is salvation received because of good works. Rather the purpose of salvation is to empower people to do good works. Col. 1:10 equates good works with walking "in a manner worthy of the Lord, fully pleasing to him, bearing fruit in every good work and increasing in the knowledge of God." Good works by Christians are seen as a participation in the work of Christ to reconcile all things to God (1:10; 2:13-16). Liberation from the powers of death restores mankind to God's original purpose of his children as doers of good works. Failure to do good works is indicative of an on-going walk in death and rebellion against God.

## Theology: How we understand God

In the previous lessons we did an exercise, reading the scripture, asking the question: How do these verses help us to understand Messiah Jesus. Now let's do the same question asking about our understanding of God. How do these verses help us to understand who God is, what is his work and how he relates to us. This list is drawn from chapters 1 and 2. I have not listed every statement pertaining to God in the two chapters, but most are here, enough to give us an appreciation for the magnitude of God's power and grace and a sketch of his plan to rescue and redeem his creation. Reading the scripture in this manner is an important skill for the Bible student to develop.

## Chapter 1

v. 4 He chose us to be in Christ, enabling us to be holy and blameless before him.
v. 5 He predestined and willed that we should be his adopted sons.
v. 7 In him we have redemption through the blood of Christ.
v. 8 His grace has been lavished upon us because of his wisdom and insight.
v. 9 He has made known to us his mission for Christ.

v. 10 His eternal plan is to unite all things in heaven and earth under the Lordship of Christ.

## Chapter 2

v. 4 He is rich in mercy towards us because of his great love for us.

v. 5 He made us alive together with Christ.

v. 6 He raised us up with Christ and seated us in the heavenly places with Christ.

v. 7 Through the coming ages he shows us his immeasurable riches of grace and kindness.

v. 10 We are his workmanship, created for good works, in which we walk.

v. 16 We have been reconciled to God, along with other peoples, into a single body.

v. 19 His household is composed only of fellow citizen-saints from many people groups.

v. 22 We the redeemed, are a holy temple, a dwelling place for God through the Spirit.

As you read and reread these statements about God, what are the pictures, understandings and impressions you begin to form about him? What changes or adjustments is the Spirit inviting you to make in your perception of God?

For myself, I am impressed by the oneness of mission: the Father and the Son, Messiah Jesus. They are joined together for the salvation and re-creating of God's universe. I see an infinitely gracious, merciful, loving God in wild pursuit of his cherished, adopted sons and daughters, eager to share with us the blessings of his eternal kingdom, the new heaven and new earth.

## A historical sidetrack

Africans have high respect for their elders because the elders, in their worldview, have a much longer tenure with the historical record of why things are as they are. It is that long-term view that endows the elderly with wisdom. That's why I so much enjoy this season of my life among Africans! So, indulge me a bit of *eldering*:

When I grew up in the U.S. during the 1940s and '50s, we were still in the twilight, the closing years, of a great debate among Protestant Christians that had been in full force during the first half of the twentieth century. On the right were the doctrinaire Calvinist, conservative, biblical literalists. To the left were the social gospel folks and liberal, humanistic theologians who taught that the Bible was a collection of folkloric and ancient myths. In those years it was important for one to line up behind one camp or the other.

The conservative group understood God as, first and foremost, a holy, righteous judge. An angry, offended deity because of the sinful depravity of man and the ruin of his creation, he would, at the moment least suspected, bring fire and brimstone vengeance against the rebelliousness of man. The quest of lost mankind was to find an escape route from the wrath of God Almighty. For God, they taught us, the only way His righteous anger could be satisfied was through the death of his perfect Son, Jesus Christ. This, the Father caused to happen in the violent death of Jesus on Calvary.

In order to get saved under this regime, one first of all needed to be among the elect, those predestined to be saved. Secondly, one had to mentally and emotionally accept that he had been declared righteous because of his election. With that, the transaction was eternally and indelibly done in the books of heaven. Finished. Little or nothing had been required on the part of the believer, and little was expected of him following the divine transaction because the verdict was irreversible. There were few worries about one's own personal righteousness, flawed as it might be, because when God looked at a person's life, He saw only the exterior cover of the righteousness of the perfect Christ. It was a convenient, rationalistic theology; specially tailored to the world view of enlightened, materialistic, individualistic North Americans.

The Protestants of this conservative theology maintained a vigorous overseas evangelistic program, particularly in Africa. Thousands dedicated their lives to propagating this version of gospel on the African continent. Traveling about West Africa I see vestiges of this theology, how it has played out in both mainline dominations and African-initiated churches. This perhaps helps us to understand the shallow, frequently misguided and even bizarre expressions of Christianity in West Africa. I'm not saying the conservative theology is to blame, but clearly it does lurk in the background in the life of West African Christianity.

Nevertheless, in my travels around West Africa, I find reason for hope. I am regularly bumping into believers in West Africa who are authentically and diligently searching for the radical, Christ-centered, apostolic expression of Christian community. The vision for this Ephesians study is to facilitate us in that very quest.

## Transform our lives

In what ways is Eph. 2 calling us to transformation? May we listen carefully to what the Spirit is saying about ways God yet needs to bring us change and new life. Review the first 3 verses of chapter 2, pondering life in the absence of the blessings of God's goodness and righteousness. It is a sordid miserable life, dominated by the prince of the power of the air, living by the passions of the flesh and culminating in a grand finale of wrath. For those who have experienced the benefits of "but God, rich in mercy" transformation, with our feet set securely on the narrow path that leads to life, what is our relationship, our attitude towards those behind us still following the course of the world on the broad road to destruction?

One option is to create distance between ourselves and those who have yet to come to the "but God" juncture. In this scenario we establish ourselves in walled, artificial communities of righteousness and as much as possible separate ourselves from those still held in the captivity of Satan, creating a literal and extreme version of "Therefore go out from their midst, and be separate from them, says the Lord, and touch no unclean thing" (2 Cor. 6:17).

In one region where I spent several years as a pioneer missionary. there were a few evangelical Christians tending to go the way of separatist communities. Unbelievers living literally next door to these folks never turned to the evangelicals for help in times of emergency and disaster. Their exclusiveness and peculiarity made it difficult for neighbors to even approach them. One day a five-year-old child, of an unbeliever's family fell into the fire pit and sustained serious burns over much of her body. The tragedy happened literally within meters of the Christian community. The Christians offered no aid or solace to the family. No one even went seeking their aid. After two days, with the child on the verge of death, the auntie came to our mission two kilometers away in the next village, seeking help from our medical personnel. We responded immediately, even helping the family get the child to the hospital. Despite the intervention of many people the child passed away about three weeks later. Even in this situation of suffering and sadness the family had nevertheless been touched with mercy and the love of God. In no way would I belittle the value of the 2 Corinthians text, but in applying a text such as that we need to look at the whole counsel of God's word. In this case, for example, we can remember John 17: 15, 16, 18: "I do not ask that you take them out of the world, but that you keep them from the evil one. They are not of the world, just as I am not of the world. As you sent me into the world, so I have sent them into the world."

Now, we return to Ephesians 2 and the thought that we, along with Christ, have been recreated to a new life, a new way of being and living even as we continue life in this world. The best way to understand our new life is that it has been recreated specifically and exclusively to be doing the good works God has ordained for us to be doing, even before the foundation of the world. Those good works are to be carbon copy of the works Jesus did in his life as he lived among people because these good works give people space to participate in the mercy and righteousness of God. Moreover, the good works demonstrate to the evil powers their defeat in face of the power of love. This is the very reason why the mission I pioneered found us in a region where people had little or no access to medical care. When there are health problems, they turn for aid to the evil powers to whom they are so completely enslaved. Our mission, wherever we find ourselves, is to be doing the good works for which we have been re-created, embracing and welcoming the unclean so they too may know and enjoy the blessings of being in God's kingdom even here on earth.

## Created for good works

If you want to know what good works you should be doing, look at the people around you who are still living by "the spirit that is now at work in the sons of disobedience and carrying out the desires of the body and the mind."

If some are experiencing strife and violence, try to help them be reconciled to their enemies.

If some are suffering health problems, help them discover lifestyle issues they could change to give better health.

If some lack ways of earning income, help them find a trade or small business opportunity.

If some are lonely and abandoned by their family, be a friend and support to them.

If some are in a broken marital relationship, help them to be reconciled or come to a place of peace and wholeness in their relationships.

If some are illiterate, help them learn to read and write.

If some are depressed and discouraged, help them find hope and joy.

This list is endless. God has redeemed and rescued you from a life outside of his kingdom; now he is asking you to simply share your peace and wholeness with those who continue to suffer because of their lostness. If you do these things, you will be doing the good works God has ordained for you when he raised you with Christ re-creating you with his workmanship.

Some people think good works are getting all dressed up and going to church on Sunday morning, singing in the choir, tithing, participating in Bible studies, dancing in worship and washing the pastor's car. Those are all things Africans expect of typical Christians, but they are not good works. They are just things you do to make yourself feel religious and pious.

Good works are things that take the disciple of Jesus out of his heavenly context into the real world where people are suffering, living in misery and the awful consequences of life apart from God. Good works are taking God's love, mercy and transforming power into the lives of people who don't know God. Good works are the handles, tools and venues enabling you to participate in the salvation of those yet far from God.

Good works are never convenient and they almost always require suffering and sacrifice. Doing good works requires that you lay down your life for the sake of those who probably won't know or appreciate what you are doing to help them find God.

Why do disciples of Jesus dedicate their entire lives to doing good works? Because that is exactly what Jesus did for you, and as his disciple you are engaged with him in the ministry of reconciling others to God.

## Reflection, discussion, action

1. Have you had "But God" moments? Times when you are overwhelmed by God's love, and the miracle of new life in Christ and his inclusion of you in his great plan for eternity.

2. What are some of the good works for which God has recreated you?

3. Explain what the Bible often means by *pistos* (faith). What does biblical faith mean in addition to mere intellectual agreement?

4. Are you among African Christians searching for the radical Christ-centered, apostolic expression of Christian community? What changes is that search bringing to your faith and life?

# Lesson FOUR

## Walls Broken Down and a Temple Built
Ephesians 2: 11-22

### Lesson 4 Passage overview

Reading this passage, one can't help but be struck with the gospel as the gospel of peace. God's initiative in the reconciliation of mankind with himself and the reconciliation of flesh and blood with human enemies is the gospel message itself.

Christ the divine peacemaker destroys the enmity both vertically and horizontally by voluntarily giving his perfect life as a peace offering. The results of his sacrifice are twofold: he lays down his life for mankind and he gives life to those who are willing to become his disciples and be recreated in his image. As his adopted sons, we are able in this life to live to the standard of his righteous and holy expectation of us because the Holy Spirit is at the helm of our hearts and wills.

The moral law of God, which once served as a dividing wall between the chosen and the not chosen, is now fulfilled in all who become alive in him through our spiritual death and resurrection. All this is at God's initiative together with our faithful commitment to the new covenant. People, regardless of their ethnic origin, are the church, God's household and his dwelling place in the Spirit.

Significant parts of this passage were likely a hymn sung by first generations of Christians as a way of celebrating the cosmic and social reality of the peace wrought by the death and resurrection of Christ.

The passage before us is one of the most significant texts on biblical peace. Someone has remarked that peace is not at the heart of the gospel—it is the gospel. These verses bear out that assertion. Here the central figure is Christ who gives his life for universal peace in the heavenlies, between earth and heaven and on the earth itself.

## Open our minds commentary and notes

*Vv 11-12 Therefore remember that at one time you Gentiles in the flesh, called "the uncircumcision" by what is called the circumcision, which is made in the flesh by hands---remember that you were at that time separated from Christ, alienated from the commonwealth of Israel and strangers to the covenants of promise, having no hope and without God in the world.*

These verses are directed at two very different ethnic groups: Gentile believers, the uncircumcised, as the outsiders and Jewish believers, the circumcised insiders. There was conflict in the church because of their ethnic differences. Jewish believers were demanding their Gentile brothers to become ethnic Jews, but Gentile believers refused to take on the Jewish identity.

Paul's message to the Jewish believers is that they, as insiders, are no better off than the outsiders because their advantage was based only on a mark made in the flesh by the hands of men; it has nothing to do with an inherent righteousness. In the

Jewish view, Gentiles were hopelessly outside the pale of God's goodness and promises. Gentiles were excluded from the people who would produce the Messiah and thus excluded from all the blessings and benefits of the Messiah.

Paul maintains that neither group had reason to boast or feel itself better than the other. God's peace is offered equally to his wayward chosen people as well as to those totally outside and alienated from hope. Paul's message is that both groups have been brought together in one body by the sacrificial blood of Christ and their resurrection together with Christ into one new re¬creation.

*Vv 13-17 But now in Christ Jesus you who once were far off have been brought near by the blood of Christ. For he himself is our peace, who has made us both one and has broken down in his flesh the dividing wall of hostility by abolishing the law of commandments expressed in ordinances, that he might create in himself one new man in place of the two, so making peace, and might reconcile us both to God in one body through the cross, thereby killing the hostility. And he came and preached peace to you who were far off and peace to those who were near.*

"But now" (similar to the "but God" of v.4) all the distance, the exclusion, enmity and separation have vanished because of the sacrificial blood of Christ. Those who once were viewed as without, strangers and hopeless have now been brought into the inner circle of God's blessings, promises and covenants.

In these verses we see the Messianic peacemaker, the Prince of Peace (Isa.9:6) both as the reconciler who brings enemies together and as the warrior who breaks, abolishes and kills that which caused the original division. Messiah (God with us) in the death of his flesh becomes a cosmic peacemaker. His death and resurrection have healed the division between heaven and earth.

When we understand this far reaching, cosmic implication of Messiah Jesus as the divine peacemaker, it becomes easier for us to understand how he breaks down the social, political and ethnic divisions among earthbound mankind. All this belongs to the Christological vision of Eph. 1:10 "to unite all things in him, things in heaven and things on earth." Surely, if Messiah's death and resurrection bring unity and peace among the powers of the cosmos, they can bring peace between Jews and Gentiles or, for that matter, any other human condition of relational enmity and division.

The phrase that Christ has abolished "the law of commandments expressed in ordinances" generates a fair amount of discussion. In terms of the law, did Christ obliterate the entire law wiping the slate totally clean? Most commentators understand Christ to have abolished only the law as "expressed in the ordinances;" that which had been added to the law, the elaborate ceremonial regulations that served to separate the Jews as an ethnic group from the Gentiles—for example, food laws, sanitation laws and circumcision.

Col. 2:14 is a helpful reference on this point: the Gentiles are received as God's people through his "canceling the record of debt that stood against us with its legal demands. This he set aside, nailing it to the cross." God cancelled the debt standing against us for our failure to keep the multitude of regulations. Gentiles are now freely able to be grafted in alongside God's chosen people with this debt being erased by the cross of Christ. Both the ethnic regulations and the incurred debt have been eternally obliterated.

## God's law in our hearts

To this empowering thought we can add the encouragement of Paul writing to both Jewish and Gentile believers in 2 Cor. 3:3: "You show that you are a letter from Christ delivered by us, written not with ink but with the Spirit of the living God, not on tablets of stone but on tablets of human hearts." Here Paul echoes the promise of Jer. 31:31: "the covenant that I will make with the house of Israel after those days, declares the Lord: I will put my law within them, and I will write it on their hearts. And I will be their God, and they shall be my people." The new man is now able to be a faithful covenant keeper because the law, God's framework for holy living, is written on his heart, the heart God intended us to have long before the walls were built.

From this we understand Jews and Gentiles to be equal beneficiaries of the new creation made possible through Messiah Jesus. And in the best sense we are no longer two but one chosen, holy people of God, empowered to faithfulness because God's standard of holiness is now inscribed on our hearts, the very seat of our will and desire. From the heart emanate our actions, the good works for which we have been created. Because our hearts are recreated into the righteousness and holiness of God, we do not need the fences (regulations) to keep us brilliantly reflecting the image of God. Praise the Lord!

While we rejoice in the union we have with Christ as God's people because the hostility has been abrogated, the real life application of this peace is not easy for most Christians. Peace is not fostered or valued in many churches because church is understood as a collection of singular individuals, each maintaining their own private peace arrangement with God. The reasoning is that having things settled with God is really all that counts. This heresy gives space for us to continue in enmity and broken relations with those around us.

But the peacemaking by Messiah Jesus is universal and all-encompassing, on heaven and on earth, for now and for the ages yet to come. All enmity, hatred and pride propelled divisions are reconciled in Christ.

In American churches it's not easy to preach peace. When you are the world's only superpower and control much of the world's wealth, that position must be maintained by spending trillions to protect it. American evangelical Christians are among the most vocal and active in supporting the military machine that keeps the U.S. solidly in the number one position. They willingly sacrifice their sons and daughters on the altar of U.S. military supremacy, believing it is God-ordained. Over half of the U.S. multi-trillion dollar annual budget goes for the cost of current and past wars the U.S. has engaged in.

### African peacemakers

When I came to Africa and began to share the story of Jesus and gospel of peace, I was amazed at the way Africans picked up on Jesus as peace. Some new believers told me how happy they were just to be at peace with each other and realize the peace and togetherness of the community of Christ. Others expressed joy at being released from the cycle of violence where one uses curses to heap evil for evil on one's enemies. They joyfully return good for evil after being set free from the heaviness of multiplying evil.

Being people of Christ's peace means they will no longer perpetuate inter-tribal conflicts, no more fights between families and no more disdain for those with a skin color lighter or darker than their own and no more aggression between men and women. No more separation because of wealth, education, religious preferences and political inclinations.

The old enmities inherited from our ancestors die hard. Are we willing to accept that Christ has broken down all those walls? If the new reality is not written on our hearts, then we keep the dividing walls because in them we find our identity. If we will hang on to the old divisions, it will not be possible to for us to flourish in God's new order of peace.

We rejoice to be received into the inheritance as God's adopted sons, a peace initiated by the loving Father; his peace does not abrogate our ethnic identity, but it does enable us to live free of the enmity and hatred that has traditionally demarcated our ethnic, social and faith identities. We can't have it both ways. The peace Christ has made between us and the Father cannot be realized in the absence of peace and oneness in all of life's social relationships. Enmity in human relations is a violation of God's design for mankind and all of creation.

But what about those we meet who do not accept the peace of Messiah Jesus, who are still living according to the desires of the flesh and are submitted to the dominion of powers which oppose Christ? For those on the outside looking in, the door to the community of Christ is always open; we welcome them in to be among us to experience and benefit from the peace and reconciliation of Christ. We offer a non-coercive invitation to be part of the family. This is real evangelism in its simplest, most authentic dress. Real evangelism doesn't work if we are busy maintaining the walls that define and divide us. The peace Jesus made on the cross came at a very high cost: his blood. That sets the reconciliation template for us. Our work of evangelical peacemaking comes at the price of sacrificing and laying down our lives for both those close and those far away from God. Other places in this study we note Jesus as the model for living. He is likewise our model in death. That's the kind of life Jesus had in mind when he said, "If anyone would come after me, let him deny himself and take up his cross daily and follow me" (Luke 9:23).

Vv. 19-22 So then you are no longer strangers and aliens, but you are fellow citizens with the saints and members of the household of God, built on the foundation of the apostles and prophets, Christ Jesus himself being the cornerstone, in whom the whole structure, being joined together, grows into a holy temple in the Lord. In him you also are being built together into a dwelling place for God by the Spirit.

These last four verses of chapter 2 have several allusions to a building, a holy place, a home dwelling, and a family household. The setting is a home-coming, a return from exile, and alien strangers being welcomed as residents and citizens with full rights. We hear of saints which should mean all the holy ones, human and angelic, who are now welcomed into the presence of God. It is the power of Christ's peace that makes this new body a living reality, now and in the ages to come. Former enemies are here joined into one great family of harmony and love.

Our study of Ephesians focuses on three major biblical themes: theology, Christology and ecclesiology. These final four verses are quite instructive in our understanding of ecclesiology, that is the church.

## What is church?

From these verses we are able to form a definition of church: It is a body of reconciliation, a venue for peacemaking, populated by former enemies, now reconciled with each other, joined together with Christ in the task of bringing all things together under his authority and recreating all things according to the eternal plan of divine perfection.

The image here is of a work-in-progress, a corporate entity rather than a fusion of individual believers. In the church more and more stones are joined into an expanding structure. New sacred space is being created as the gospel of peace embraces more and more former enemies into a temple worthy of the God of peace.

The instruction of chapter 2 is to help us understand that the church is made up of social groups that were formerly defined by high walls of enmity and separation: Jews, Gentiles, Africans, Americans, rich, poor, male, female, illiterate, university graduates, farmers, doctors, clergy, laity, conservatives, liberals, high church, low church, the perfect, the deformed and dozens more pigeonholes we have for identifying, qualifying and valuing people. With all those walls broken down and the hostility killed, these have been brought together as a holy temple witnessing to the power and the supremacy of Christ and the righteousness of God.

Verse 20 provides three elements that make church the authentic organism Christ the head intends it to be: It must be built on the foundation of the apostles and prophets, Christ Jesus himself being the cornerstone. For the church today to be a faithful model of what the head, Christ, inaugurated 2000 years ago, Christ must be the cornerstone on which it rests, along with the rest of the foundation: the first century apostles and prophets.

The apostles and prophets are those who were present with Christ during his earthly ministry. Because of their proximity to him, they were able to catch a vision and understanding of him and his mission in ways those of us of later generations are unable to do. Empowered by Holy Spirit wisdom and understanding, these apostles and prophets were qualified to be in on the inauguration of the earthly community we know as the church of Jesus Christ.

In this building the focus is on the cornerstone, Christ. It is in and through Christ that the whole structure is joined together and grows into the holy temple worthy of God's presence. Lacking this cornerstone or having an inadequate understanding of the cornerstone, the structure is weakened and will fall unless it is somehow artificially propped up.

In order for the church to continue the work of Christ and accomplish God's kingdom coming to earth as it is in heaven, the community of Christ needs to have a spirit of radicalism. Being radical simply means going back to the roots. Every generation of Christians needs the renewal and refreshment that comes by going back to this foundation laid for us by Christ the chief cornerstone and his first century apostles and prophets. (It is the author's hope that the study material you have in your hands right now will encourage you to this very radicalism.) Lacking that renewal, a secondary foundation slowly inserts itself between the current believers and the authentic foundation: an accretion of traditions, doctrines and ordinances that may have seemed so right when they were inaugurated but for future generations mean almost nothing and are like a short circuit that slowly but surely drains away the power of the dynamic foundation.

Returning to the foundation enables us to be disciples of Christ in a way that makes our faith and life an adequate, relevant expression of the life of Christ for our time and cultural setting.

I have made numerous bicycle tours of Western Europe. When I am in that part of the world, one of my favorite things to do is to leave the busy highway and slip quietly into the sacred space of a building that has been a house of worship for many, many generations of Christians. Amid the soaring pillars and exquisite stained glass, I am able to understand better the spirituality of people who had their appointed time on earth hundreds of years before mine. I love the art and architecture of these ancient edifices.

But most of what I see in these hushed enclaves makes me scratch my head trying to imagine what Jesus would make of all the accoutrements. The images, burial coffins, urns of holy water, glitzy altars, rows of empty benches and flickering candles bear little or no connection to anything I read about the suffering servant of Nazareth who went about touching people with God's healing love and preaching peace, freedom, justice and eternal life for the poor and downtrodden. I wrestle with the puzzling question: how does one get from the Jesus who blessed the little children, opened the eyes of the blind, raised a widow's son, said he is among us as one who serves and, for doing that, was tortured to death by the religious-political establishment—how is the great Jesus event somehow all reduced to this lifeless, tradition-encrusted monument?

How this aberration of Prince of Peace came to be is for the same reason the aberrations of West African Christianity are so common and why Jews of Jesus' time were religious and at the same time far from what God had planned for his chosen people. When believers do not go back to build on the foundation of the apostles and prophets with Jesus himself as the chief cornerstone, they end up with a formal, institutionalized religion only remotely resembling the original.

While it is important for us to learn from our predecessors, our life of faith is about a relationship with the living Lord of the church. Traditions are a part of being human. Traditions provide markers, defining our lives and giving us identity and a sense of direction. But traditions and passed-on cultural values need scrutiny and critiquing by the covenant we have made with God. First and foremost, our covenant is to be disciples of Christ and to join God in the grand plan of bringing all things in heaven and on earth under the authority of Christ.

Paul valued his Jewish heritage but, relative to the value of his commitment to the Lord, he says, "I count everything as loss because of the surpassing worth of knowing Christ Jesus my Lord." Thus, we are not here to toss all the traditions and cultural markers out the window, but they do need to be critiqued against the ultimate value of life: being re-created into the likeness of Jesus Christ, the great Lord of time and eternity.

For our congregations we have a list of ten values, the last of which deals with this very question: We are ready to challenge the values and practices of our culture wherein they violate the Spirit and teachings of Jesus. We don't allow the world (our culture) to squeeze us into its mold when that mold diminishes Christlikeness in ourselves or others.

## Transform our lives

We have already agreed that Jesus is the model for our lives. What he did, we will do. As he was in this world, so are we. As the second, perfect Adam, he did what the first Adam was unable to do: to glorify God and manifest the righteousness of God on earth in the way he conducted his life. That is precisely the same vision God has for us, the followers of Jesus: to glorify him in the way we live and become visible, corporal examples of his righteousness every single day by the way we conduct our lives.

The primary focus of Christ's mission is to make peace at all levels, terrestrial and celestial, between God and man and among the social community of mankind. There's nothing in the entire universe that is not transformed by the peace of Christ where he is acknowledged as Lord. Moreover, everyone who is in Christ is a full time peacemaker.

In West Africa that is a daunting assignment. In this culture it is difficult to find social interaction that is not powered by animosity, a desire to control the other, intimidation and aggression.

Little children scarcely knee-high to an adult will walk up to one of their age mates and POW! Peacemaking is not even on the screen for most people. We learn to be combative and confrontive from little on up.

Can West African Christians be transformed into pro¬active peacemakers? Can we be the people of God's peace on this continent? Can we become the people in our communities who enable enemies to become reconciled to God and to each other? Can we preach peace to those who are near and to those who are far beyond the covenant of peace? Can we knock down the walls that divide? Absolutely, we can and we will, as we allow God to transform us into his people of peace.

Just start your peacemaking career at home in your family relationships, then, move beyond to co-workers, friends and the people you worship with and hang out with. Very quickly the word will spread that you are an active peacemaker in the community of Christ.

In virtually every election in Africa, the candidates will promise peace because they know peace is one of the most longed-for realities among Africans. Few politicians are able to deliver on their promises, but as Christian peacemakers, we can.

## Keys to becoming a Christian peacemaker

With these five perspectives on life, peacemaking will come naturally and willingly:

1. **Trust in the absolute faithfulness of God to keep and save in spite of adversity, aggression of others and threats of violence** (Psa. 25:10, 1 Cor. 1:9). God is the Alpha and the

Omega, the begiining and the end. He is always there and always will be. God is dependable and faithful beyond what we are even able to comprehend. When people are not secure in the eternal loving care of God they will find it nessecary to fight for their rights, take revenge and control others.

2. **Leave vengance to the Lord.** Rom. 12:17-21 God is the only one who can judge with absolute justice. He alone has the ability to compensate evil in a way that is final and just. If we attempt to take revenge, we then participate in evil, using evil to do something we are not qualified and designed to do. When we entrust God with taking care of the compensation we are freed to return good for evil so that we oursleves do not become controlled by evil. Our responsibility when offended is to do good to the one who has wronged us.Doing good is a powerful witness, giving our enemy opportunity to be confronted by the love of God.

3. **Lay down and lose our lives for the sake of Christ and his Kingdom.** This saying of Jesus is in all four gospels, signifying its importance in the life of the first century church. (Matt. 10:39, Mark 8:35, Luke 17:33, John 12;25) We have the choice of having everything we need or desire in this life, but in finding all life has to offer means loss of life to come.

4. **Finding the life that matters ultimately** means we hold lightly onto the material and social advantages of this life and in so doing we experience the peace that comes with casting all our anxieties on him for,"after you have suffered a little while, the God of all grace, who has called you to his eternal glory in Christ, will himself restore, confirm, strengthen, and establish you" (1 Peter 5; 7, 10)

5. **Suffering is normal for the Christian.** (2 Tim. 3:12-14; Matt 5:11-12; 1 Peter 2:20-21) Peacemaking may put us in a position of vulnerability and risk just as it did for Jesus. As we join him in his great task of breaking down walls that divide people, we are prepared to suffer with him for the sake of peace between peoples and between God and mankind.

6. **Have an eschatological perspective on life.** We live with our eyes on the world to come where we will eternally be with the glorified Christ and where at the name of Jesus every knee should bow, in heaven and on earth and under the earth, and every tongue confess that Jesus Christ is Lord, to the glory of God the Father" (Phil. 2: 10-11).

## Reflection, discussion, action

1. What walls still exist between Christians and between unbelievers and Christians that Christ has broken down? How will your life change when the walls are removed?

2. How could the African church move forward to challenge the cultural barriers of what's up and what's down? What do we do about barriers that diminish Christlikeness in ourselves and others?

3. What role do you see the church filling as peacemakers in conflictive situations in Africa?

4. Which of the keys to becoming a peacemaker do you find the most difficult?

# Lesson FIVE

## The Revelation of God's Mystery of the Ages
Ephesians 3: 1-13

### Lesson 5 Passage overview

In this lesson Paul establishes his apostleship credentials because he has been chosen as a special messenger to make known the mystery concerning the Gentiles. It is he who has been chosen to reveal that God's salvation is open to all regardless of their ethnic background. Paul is a prisoner, in a good sense, as the carrier of that message of hope. He may also have been a prisoner of the Roman government at this writing.

Verse 1 is an incomplete sentence providing opportunity for a digression in which he reviews again the mystery and the fact that he is the designated apostle of that message. The digression runs from v.2 through v.7 stating Paul's credentials as the messenger. The message is that the Gentiles are now fully included in the body of God's chosen people and have become heirs to all of the Messianic hopes and promises.

Verses 8-12 repeat the thoughts of vv. 2-7 with a cosmic perspective on the role the church has in the mystery of putting heavenly powers on notice that God's wisdom and plan are for the salvation of all of his creation.

The section concludes with a plea for his readers not to lose heart over his sufferings for the sake of the gospel and his apostolic commission.

In this first half of chapter 3, Paul speaks again of the mystery of God, hidden for ages but now revealed. Paul, of all the apostles, was the one designated to disclose the mystery, and it is he who was most influential in the realization of the mystery. A significant point in these verses is the model of church leadership and missionary we see in the apostle Paul, a magnificent example of a church leader giving himself totally to the propagation the gospel in a spirit of great humility even though his authority and influence was unparalleled.

The mystery, briefly, is that the time had now arrived when non-Jewish people could, on a large scale, become part of the peoplehood of God and this on an equal footing with the original Jewish chosen people, benefiting of all the promises and covenants God had made with the descendants of Jacob. Because Christ broke down the wall, all mankind, regardless of ethnic background, is now graciously welcomed into the community of the "one new man"' relationship with God.

This section of verses goes on to describe the role the new chosen community has in the mission of God, witnessing to cosmic forces of His power and wisdom to gather up all things in Christ for time and eternity.

*Vv. 1-7 For this reason I, Paul, a prisoner for Christ Jesus on behalf of you Gentiles---assuming that you have heard of the stewardship of God's grace that was given to me for you, how the mystery was made known to me by revelation, as I have written briefly. When you read this, you can perceive my insight into the mystery of Christ, which was not made known to the sons of men in other generations as it has now been revealed to his holy apostles and prophets by the Spirit. This mystery is that the Gentiles are fellow heirs, members of the same body, and partakers of the promise in Christ Jesus through the gospel. Of this gospel I was made a minister according to the gift of God's grace, which was given me by the working of his power.*

Paul introduces himself as one who has a momentous insight of revelation into the mystery of Christ, yet at the same time he is a prisoner for Christ Jesus suffering in a filthy prison cell for the gospel. He draws attention to this situation as a signal of his non-status. In contrast, in the current African scheme of things, one who had been specially chosen to receive revelation of one the great mysteries of God for all ages would bear a title of divinity such as His Worship, the most Excellent, Right Reverend Doctor such and such. He most certainly would insist on being clothed in a splendid robe and ensconced on a plush red throne-like chair in a magnificent cathedral.

By contrast, Paul's secondary message is about how God carries on the work of his kingdom through the weak, the suffering, the humble and the despised. These are the ones who are chosen and empowered to do the great work of proclaiming God's salvation.

Paul's realistic self-perception is that of a steward or administrator of God's plan to include the Gentiles together with Jews as God's holy ones. He sees himself as being among the foundational apostles and prophets together with Christ, the cornerstone (2:20). Paul, as a servant in God's household, is an agent of the peace wrought by the death and glorification of Christ. This gift of being a servant of the gospel is accompanied and carried forward by God's power, in striking contrast to the fact that Paul is at this very time a helpless, confined prisoner of Rome. But in spite of Paul's limitations and weakness, God's salvation is making great bounds forward.

All this is crucial and directional for us who today carry on the work of proclaiming, facilitating and administering this same gospel in Africa. Starting with first century foundation of Christianity, the in-breaking of God's kingdom came through humble, suffering, self-sacrificing servant leaders, Messiah Jesus himself being our prime example. The same is true in Africa today.

By contrast, today we see among those who would claim the title of 'leadership' in the church of Africa are would-be potentates on par with the big-men politicians who demand the groveling adulation, subjection, servanthood and obedient service of their subjects. That's normal if one is building a worldly, institutionalized kingdom, but it doesn't work in the economy of the living body of Jesus Christ.

In God's program, the principle is that one starts by taking the lowest seat, as Jesus said: "But when you are invited [to a wedding feast], go and sit in the lowest place, so that when your host comes he may say to you, Friend, move up higher. Then you will be honored in the presence of all who sit at table with you. For everyone who exalts himself will be humbled, and he who humbles himself will be exalted" (Luke 14:10-11). Also, "Clothe yourselves, all of you, with humility toward one another, for "God opposes the proud but gives grace to the humble. Humble yourselves, therefore, under the mighty hand of God so that at the proper time he may exalt you" (1 Peter 5:5-6)

Would that all church leaders in Africa could say with Paul, "I have learned in whatever situation I am to be content. I know how to be brought low, and I know how to abound. In any and every circumstance, I have learned the secret of facing plenty and hunger, abundance and need. I can do all things through him who strengthens me (Phil. 4: 11-13).

As we contemplate the suffering and humility of our foundation, Christ and his apostles, we need to count the cost of what it is going to mean for us to follow them in making known the saving wisdom and power of God to the African continent. A second challenge before us is the shape of the gospel of peace on a continent fraught with racism, ethnic conflict and a minority power elite holding sway over the impoverished masses. This challenge is closely related to the above discussion of finding one's place at the back of the line. Many church leaders aim at a place of prestige and elitism, thereby rebuilding the walls that Christ has broken down, walls that divide people into social and economic class.

I am aware of churches in Africa who bar the poor from church functions and worship because they are not properly dressed. Any church that doesn't welcome the poor, even if they are dressed in rags, needs to stop using the name of Christ in any association with that church. Refusing to receive the poor, for any reason, is an affront and denial of Jesus Christ. It negates the sacrifice of his life, since in his death he destroyed those very barriers between people. Far be it from the church bearing his name, Messiah Jesus, to reestablish the barrier walls that divide people for whatever reason.

One time I had a conversation with a brother from Congo (Kinshasa), a member of one of the churches with a clear peace theology in that blood-drenched country. His statement was that the peace churches offer the only hope for Congo because it is there where people caught in conflict cease to be enemies and are able to meet together in peace and love. What a magnificent testimony to the barrier-breaking power of Christ!

## Ethnic conflict in the first-century church

Paul's monumental pronouncement of verses 1-7 "that the Gentiles are fellow heirs, members of the same body, and partakers of the promise in Christ Jesus through the gospel" in today's context hardly raises a ripple. To that assertion in today's society, people's reaction is "say what?" Of course, Gentiles are members of the same body and partakers...why would one ever suggest they were not? But during the first 150 years of church history this was a very big issue. Many early Christians believed that to be part of God's chosen people it was required that one first become an ethnic Jew. Paul's explosive message was that the Gentiles becoming faithful followers of Jesus are welcomed into God's household just as they are: ethnic Gentiles.

At its beginning the Christian church was almost exclusively a Jewish sect. Nearly everyone participating in the church during the first decades of the church's existence was a Jew. Jesus and all his disciples were Jews, and most of the people they ministered to were Jews. On the day of Pentecost when the crowd gathered to witness the outpouring of the Holy Spirit and listen to the sermon of Peter, the crowd were devout Jewish people gathered in Jerusalem "from every nation under heaven" (Acts 2:5).

It wasn't until Paul's conversion and the subsequent inauguration of his missionary activities among both Jews and Gentiles around the Mediterranean that significant numbers of converts to Christianity were Gentiles. Prior to that, among the Jewish majority it was assumed that to be a follower of Christ one also needed to be an ethic Jew. Gentiles were welcomed into the church, but only as they were proselytized to the Jewish faith. That is, males needed to be circumcised, various cleanliness rituals practiced, food regulations observed as well as the celebrating of Jewish holidays.

As time went on, it became evident that the Gentiles were responding to the gospel and that they were experiencing transforming faith in Christ without becoming Jews. At the Jerusalem leadership council in 49 AD, most of the Jewish regulations and requirements were dropped for Gentile converts. Nevertheless, a powerful and vocal faction of Jewish leaders in the church continued to envision the church as a Jewish Messianic sect. Three decades after Pentecost, the church was experiencing a raging controversy over this question. In the church of Rome the battle between the Jewish traditionalists and the Gentile new comers had degenerated into the two sides shouting obscenities at each other!

The apostle Paul attempted to bring peace to the church on this issue through his epistles, especially during the fifth and sixth decades AD. His message was built on the belief that Abraham, father of all the faithful, is the example of all mankind who come into covenant with God. Abraham's covenant was validated by nothing more or less than his relationship of trust and obedience to God. This is an eternal principle of God. We become part of his people, his promises and covenants through the faithfulness of Jesus Christ and our faithful commitment to be his disciples.

Circumcision, ritual purity, food laws, holy days and the like serve the purpose of demarcating an ethnic people group, but they have no validity in terms of bringing one into a saving, transforming relationship with God. Those practices served the purpose of providing an identity for the people through whom the Messiah would come. With Messiah Jesus' faithfulness and glorification, all those ethnic distinctions became obsolete. One new people, those who are committed to doing the will of God, the brothers and sisters of our Lord, are now one chosen people of God regardless of their ethnic origin.

The Jewish believer versus Gentile believer conflict never was totally resolved but it eventually became moot because of growing anti-Semitism in the church. The Jews ceased participation in the Jesus movement and the problem withered.

For Paul's teaching to impact us today in the place of Gentile we need to substitute words like poor, uncivilized, uneducated, illiterate, HIV positive, beggar, lazy or the name of a tribe which we don't appreciate. We still have difficulty accepting other believers equally if they have a social or economic designation different from our own. The point of Paul's revelation is that Jesus, in his defeat of the powers, has swept away any and all barriers in the new community of God's household. The playing field of the church is level. We are an egalitarian body serving each other and the world with our gifts so that together we might all attain to the fullness of Christ.

## Our priority: focused on Christ or maintaining the boundaries?

Yet another important teaching from these verses is the priority of focusing on our center, Jesus Christ, rather than on the boundaries. True, we do need boundaries: thus far and no further or this and this are non-negotiable Christian standards. However, a church can expend most of its time and energy policing the boundaries to the extent that we have no energy left to do our real mission of bringing hope and healing to our broken world. It seems the more energy we put into maintaining the fences, the more furiously we need to work at it!

It is right, for example, that churches have the standard that our youth maintain sexual abstinence prior to marriage. But we can get so consumed in the enforcement of that principle and disciplining the violators that we neglect to build the image and power of Christ in our youth, which, in the end, is the only way they are empowered to wait until marriage.

Christian life standards pertaining to our sexuality, our social-economic relationships or what we do in our leisure activities are far easier to maintain when we are equipped with the Spirit of Christ within that makes us totally committed to doing only that which brings worship and honor to God's immutable holiness. When the law of God is written on our hearts (Jeremiah 31:31), there is the power of God's Spirit within us that slams shut the door of temptation to sin. Church leaders and teachers need to focus much more on forming Christ within the hearts and spirits of the believers than to be serving as police who maintain the boundaries.

*Vv. 8-13 To me, though I am the very least of all the saints, this grace was given, to preach to the Gentiles the unsearchable riches of Christ, and to bring to light for everyone what is the plan of the mystery hidden for ages in God who created all things, so that through the church the manifold wisdom of God might now be made known to the rulers and authorities in the heavenly places. This was according to the eternal purpose that he has realized in Christ Jesus our Lord, in whom we have boldness and access with confidence through our faith in him. So I ask you not to lose heart over what I am suffering for you, which is your glory.*

Paul begins this passage by again emphasizing his humble qualifications for the great task which God has assigned him. He says this as an encouragement to each of us. God has called us to do a great work and even though our qualifications are far less than one would expect, God empowers us to do his work so that the results depend not on us but upon him. Our most important asset is simply to be available for what God wants to do through our lives.

Please note in verses 8-11 Paul's (and the church's) commission from the Lord:

1. Preaching the unsearchable riches of Christ to unbelievers, that Christ has broken down the dividing walls, bringing us peace and oneness with God and our fellow men.

    Bringing into everyone's view God's eternal plan for his creation, how through Christ and the church, he is bringing creation back to its original beauty, peace and perfection. The community of Christ, in our life together, is a foretaste in this age of the fulfilled, eternal peaceable kingdom.

2. As lives and communities are submitted and transformed into an expression of God's kingdom, we are serving notice to the powers in the heavenly realm that they also must submit to what God is doing through Christ—that is, gathering up and restoring all things under the authority of Christ. Thus it can be said that the church is an active agency, participating with God in the realization of his eternal plan.

## Cosmic principalities, powers and rulers

A phrase in this passage that raises curiosity and considerable conjecture on the part of theologians is "rulers and authorities in the heavenly places." Overall, Ephesians has numerous references to the cosmic, spiritual powers (4:27; 6:11-12; 2:2; 3:10; 1:21).

The powers can be understood as a broad spectrum of forces that are set against God and his kingdom. The understanding is broadened by the possibility that God created and ordained the powers for good and that it wasn't until the fall they became corrupted and opposed to him. This allows that, even though they are fallen, at least certain powers still have the potential of serving the purpose of bringing cohesion, form and structure to society and creation (for example civil governments, politics, institutions, economic systems and the laws and powers of nature). If powers attempt to undermine the authority of God, they are evil. If they help to hold society together and provide structure, order and justice, they are serving their God-ordained responsibilities and must be respected. We understand that all powers, evil (as most of them are) or the beneficial ones, are all to be gathered up in and under the authority of Christ (1:10). The powers likewise are being or will be transformed into God's original perfect vision for his creation.

It is to these powers that the church witnesses to the manifold, multi-varied wisdom of God as the powers see in us, the faithful church, the transforming power of the gospel even in this present evil age. In dealing with the powers, the church has a variety of avenues of witness and confrontation: prayer, exorcism, spiritual warfare, evangelism, prophetic calls for justice and active peace-making. As God gifts us, we should engage all of these tools in our witness. The community of Christ needs to stand together in this massive frontal attack on the evil powers. We need to stand with our brothers and sisters in the various ways God gifts and empowers us to demonstrate to the powers that Jesus Christ is already in charge, at least in the collective life of Jesus' disciples.

I cannot produce an exhaustive list of the strongholds, powers and authorities here in West Africa. There are probably many I am not aware of, but here are six we see regularly:

1. **Religious (including animistic) belief systems.** Most of the belief systems are boldly opposed to the Lordship of Jesus Christ and do everything in their power to thwart the king-

dom of God. Even some belief systems (churches) bearing the Christian label are not submitted to the rule and authority of Christ. Most religious belief systems in Africa are so embedded with social and world view forces that it is very difficult for persons to be set free of their darkness and come to the light of Christ. Those who do choose freedom in Christ are almost guaranteed to face stiff persecution, shaming and discrimination from their families and communities.

2. **Civil governments.** Corruption in African governments at all levels is legendary. Generally it is assumed that if one is a politician or civil servant he is raking in far more financial benefits than his salary provides. Few dollars coming into Africa from international lending agencies and non-governmental agencies, earmarked to alleviate poverty, actually reach the people they were intended to help move out of poverty. Most funds end up in the off-shore bank accounts of those handling the money, enabling a tiny minority of Africans to live at levels common among upper income folks in the West. The son of a long-term president in one West African country now sits in jail, charged with amassing an astonishing fortune of $4 billion during his father's 12 year tenure in office. Corruption is a way of life at all governmental levels. For example, there are stretches of highway in some countries that have multiple police and customs check points in the space of just a few kilometers. At each point these officials are legally able to extract fees from passersby in what amounts to little more than legalized highway robbery.

3. **Power to dominate, subjugate and control others for personal gain and prestige.** One is faced with this power stronghold at every turn in African society. It makes serious inroads even in Christian churches and organizations. Number one on most people's agenda is finding a place in the social order, a foothold where they can have others lower than themselves and gain submission and honor from those below them. The first master/servant division one learns as he grows up in African society is that males are above females. Second is my tribe is better than yours. From there the social ups and downs go on and on: fair skin is up, black is down; age is up, youth is down; Mandiago is up, Balanta is down; government job is up, farming is down; clergy are up, laity are down; tall is up, short is down and many more. One of the most tragic fruits of the up/down subjugating system is what it is doing spiritually and emotional to women. By extension, it holds captive the potential for mutuality and dignity in gender relations. Even in Christian marriages, some men continue to physically beat their wives. Family relationships which God designed to bring peace, security and freedom to develop Christlike personalities are instead characterized by fear, subjugation, repression and anger.

4. **The explotation, abuse and diminution of the natural environment.** One of the forces assuring ongoing poverty in Africa is the absence of a sense of stewardship, resposibility and care for natural resources, particularly the issue of soil management and fertility maintanace. Africa, with it's climatic and soil diversity could be feeding the rest of the world. In-

stead, per capita food production is declining and Africa is becoming more and more dependant on imported food. there is a powerful force blinding Africans to the importance of the priciples of agronomy and God's laws in caring for his creation. that power is determined to keep Africa in poverty, hunger, poor health and misery.

5. **The power of the dead to control and influence the living.** In many West African villages you won't find a community cemetery. That's because the dead are normally buried adjacent to the veranda of the house where the person had lived. This house was, for many years the house for the person; it continues to be the home of his spirit after his physical decease. This means the spirits of the ancestor are lingering on the veranda and in the yard around the house. One must be mindful to acknowledge their presence upon entering the doorway to the house. One leaves offerings and makes libations to maintain the good will of the ever present ancestral spirits. Placating offended ancestors has precedence over tending to necessities of the living like medical care and school fees for your children. When misfortune or accident visits the household, the first concern is that one of the ancestors has been offended. A visit to the jumbakuse (witch doctor) is imperative to determine what oblations need to be made to restore the good will of the spirit.

6. **A spirit of lawlessness and anarchy.** There is a prevalence of the spirit of impunity. That is, one is free to break the law, if he can manage to escape capture and the consequent punishment.

If one is killed during his attempt to rob, he is shamed; if he succeeds with the heist, he is honored. Guilt is not incurred from disobeying a law. Guilt is in getting caught. If one goes undetected he is free, even honored, for committing murder and mayhem. It is a sign of a real man to successfully steal without getting caught. In the past if a man had his eye on a potential wife in the neighborhood, her father would grant the daughter to a man who succeeded in stealing one of the father's cows. He would be a noble, brave and intrepid son-in-law if he was able to make the theft without getting shot. This may no longer be the typical pattern for getting a wife, but the driving spirit behind the anarchy and lawlessness is still alive and well in some parts of West Africa.

These are just six examples of the "rulers and authorities in the heavenly places," which dominate life in West Africa. The good news is that Jesus Christ, because of his exemplary life and subsequent glorification, has disabled these powers in the lives of his disciples. This is the manifold wisdom of God that is being made known to the rulers and authorities in the heavenly places. In the community of Christ, he alone is Lord; the rulers and authorities are no longer in charge. It is through the lives of Jesus' followers, the church, that witness and proof are put before the rulers that their power is ineffective when set alongside the power of Christ in his community. What they see now in the church is but a preview of what is going to happen when God's eternal kingdom is consummated and all will bow in servitude and worship of the Lamb. All rulers and powers opposed to righteousness will be eternally banished in God's new order.

The defeat of the powers calls us to two areas of reflection. First, go through these six powers and consider how the anti-Christ ruler and power in each case has been defeated in the daily life of the Christian. What is the evidence the lives of Christians have been transformed and no longer serve these rulers? What is the standard of God's righteousness that displaces the evil conduct of lives under the rulers?

Second, what happens when people, claiming to live under the authority of Christ, in real life are still serving the rulers and powers of this age? One of the most glaring examples of this in Africa is the extent to which many evangelical and Pentecostal church leaders are up to their ears serving the power to dominate, subjugate and control others for personal gain and prestige. This is in direct disobedience to the teaching of Christ in Matthew 20:25- 28: "But Jesus called them to him and said, 'You know that the rulers of the Gentiles lord it over them, and their great ones exercise authority over them. It shall not be so among you. But whoever would be great among you must be your servant, and whoever would be first among you must be your slave, even as the Son of Man came not to be served but to serve, and to give his life as a ransom for many.'"

When we choose to ignore the teachings and example of Christ the rulers and powers have a heyday. Instead of witnessing to them of the transforming power of Christ we are affirming our entrenched commitment to the rulers and powers of this evil age and hold our Lord up to shame and contempt (Heb. 6:6).

## The gospel and suffering

The last verse of this section, verse 13, deserves our serious reflection. Here the Apostle speaks of his suffering on behalf of the church. An important commentary on Paul's theology of suffering is found a few pages later in Colossians 1:24-29: *Now I rejoice in my sufferings for your sake, and in my flesh I am filling up what is lacking in Christ's afflictions for the sake of his body, that is, the church, of which I became a minister according to the stewardship from God that was given to me for you, to make the word of God fully known, the mystery hidden for ages and generations but now revealed to his saints. To them God chose to make known how great among the Gentiles are the riches of the glory of this mystery, which is Christ in you, the hope of glory. Him we proclaim, warning everyone and teaching everyone with all wisdom, that we may present everyone mature in Christ. For this I toil, struggling with all his energy that he powerfully works within me.*

The apostle tells the believers that preaching the good news is inseparable from suffering. Why? Because the gospel itself was forged in the flames of suffering as it became a reality for us, in the passion of Messiah Jesus. Stewards of the message of God's salvation riches suffer along with the Savior in making the message real in the lives of disciples and as witness to the powers. That is why Paul unashamedly suffers for the believers and is why evangelism today happens in the context of suffering and hardship.

Around the world today, where the gospel in making serious inroads against satanic strongholds, there is great suffering.

West Africa is no exception. Although some preachers proclaim triumphalism and prosperity, those who challenge the powers noted above suffer serious hardship and opposition. But don't lose heart because of suffering, the apostle encourages us. When there is opposition it affirms that the enemy is being challenged, threatened and overcome by the power of Christ.

## Reflection, Discussion, Action

1. Describe in some detail the mystery of Christ that was made known to Paul. Why did God keep this as a mystery until after the glorification of Christ? What problem did Paul's revelation of the mystery create in the first century church?

2. Describe some of the barrier walls in the church of West Africa today. Why must these walls come down when we have Christ as the cornerstone of the church?

3. What are the major principalities and powers which you confront regularly? How do you witness to them the victory of Christ?

4. How have you experienced or are you experiencing suffering for the gospel? Why is suffering nearly inevitable for the disciple of Christ?

# Lesson SIX

## Finding Spiritual Strength
Ephesians 3:14-21

### Lesson 6 Passage overview

Paul's epistles include prayers for the readers. This section is a prayer that highlights his concerns for the believers as they begin to absorb the majesty of God's mystery now revealed.

The first request of the prayer is for renewal and strengthening of the inner man as the message of Gentile inclusion touches the hearts of all believers. He has in mind the harm that the Jew-Gentile conflict has had on the church and their need for rooting and grounding in God's all-inclusive love.

Second, Paul prays that they might get a vision for the all comprehensive breadth and power of God as he is in the process of gathering up all things in Christ.

Third, he asks that God's very being would be present within the gathered body as he brings together former enemies and rejected peoples into one sanctified family of God.

The last verse is a doxology commending the readers to God's energizing power as he does through his church far beyond what we are even able to ask for or imagine.

The final seven verses of chapter three are an apostolic prayer Paul offers on behalf of believers in the churches. There are three requests in the prayer: one, that the believers would be renewed in their innermost being with the love and power of God's Spirit presence; two, that they would be empowered to understand the unsearchable riches of the indwelling Christ and his love; and third, that the believers would be filled to completion with the fullness of God. The prayer opens with a humble acknowledgement of God who is Father of all beings in both heaven and earth, and it concludes with a doxology giving glory to God for what he is doing through Jesus Christ and the church to accomplish the eternal purposes for his creation.

Vv. 14-21 *For this reason I bow my knees before the Father, from whom every family in heaven and on earth is named, that according to the riches of his glory he may grant you to be strengthened with power through his Spirit in your inner being, so that Christ may dwell in your hearts through faith---that you, being rooted and grounded in love, may have strength to comprehend with all the saints what is the breadth and length and height and depth, and to know the love of Christ that surpasses knowledge, that you may be filled with all the fullness of God. Now to him who is able to do far more abundantly than all that we ask or think, according to the power at work within us, to him be glory in the church and in Christ Jesus throughout all generations, forever and ever. Amen.*

## God the Father of all people groups

Paul kneels in reverence and submission before him who is Father of all people groups in both heaven and earth. We are bold enough to come to him as adopted sons with our petitions but in an attitude of honoring him as Father and head over all. Even the peoples who do not honor him as Father are under his authority. As for the "families in heaven" there is much speculation as to what they include—people who lived and died on earth? Angelic families? Families of hostile spirit beings and powers?

The fact that God has named the families is indicative of his authority and claim over them even though they may be existing in ways that are far removed from his purposes. God's saving and transforming power encompasses all entities and aspects of his creation, even those in rebellion against him, including the awesome, dark fortresses we deal with in West Africa. This is not to say that all will be ultimately saved, but that all will at some point be forced to reckon with God's righteous judgment and authority. It is in this framework of God's ultimate power that the church moves forward confidently in its task of witness to the cosmos.

## The empowering love of the indwelling Christ

Paul speaks of both Christ's dwelling within us and our dwelling in Christ, within the inner person both collectively and individually. The sense is that Christ is so much at home, within and among us, that our actions as individuals and as a church collectively represent the actions of Christ. The prayer is that Christ indwells us to such an extent that when people see our lives, they are seeing the life of Christ. Is this possible in reality?

It is easy to find examples of Christians acting according to their own fleshly desires, manifesting the same spirit and driving force one would find among unbelievers. Research in the United

States indicates that the conduct among persons professing to be Christians is virtually indistinguishable from that of unbelievers with respect to issues of justice, righteousness and morality. If this research is correct, and there is no reason to think it is not, then being either a Christian or a non-Christian has made little or no difference in the way one lives and behaves. This kind of Christian faith has been seriously compromised by powers hostile to God, the never ending goal of our ancient enemy.

In West Africa we are challenged to be so controlled by the love, power and righteousness of Christ that when people interact with us they will know they have encountered God's presence. And the powers in the heavenlies will likewise be shown that ultimate authority is in Christ. Great significance rests with the phrase of v. 17: "that Christ may dwell in your hearts by faith." One frequently hears a gimmicky invitation to a personal salvation that can happen by letting Christ into your heart, a kind of abstract spiritual event that promotes a warm, fuzzy feeling towards Jesus in some remote, obscure corner of one's being. When becoming Christian is reduced to a trifling, momentary raise-your-hand impulse, it should be no surprise that Christians are indistinguishable from non-Christians.

In v. 17 Paul is saying that Christ takes up residence in our hearts and the totality of our lives as we are crucified and die with him so that God's power resurrects from the dead, old life, a new person, recreated into the image and Spirit of Christ. The 'by faith' term is better understood as "by our living in faithfulness and obedience" to Christ who is now the Lord of our lives. See also Rom. 6:1-11 and 2 Cor. 5:14-17.

## Transform our lives

When we are living in faithfulness and obedience to Christ, now the Lord of our lives, these are some of the characteristics of our old self that have been crucified with Christ:

1. The use of physical violence against anyone for any reason.
2. Repaying evil with evil.
3. Having sexual relations with anyone other than the spouse to whom we are married and to whom we have made a lifelong commitment.
4. Taking property belonging to another person as our own without return or recompense.
5. Speaking of another person in a way that will cause those listening to unfairly devalue and lose respect for that person.
6. Speaking untruthfully or deceivingly, attempting to influence others for our gain.
7. Destroying or damaging the property of another person without proper restitution.
8. Taking advantage of the vulnerable in our society, such as children, widows, the poor and ignorant, the foreigners, and the physically or mentally disadvantaged.
9. Participating in demonic or occultic ceremonies or placing curses on others.
10. Benefitting from schemes of governmental (or NGO) corruption.
11. Becoming intoxicated to the point where our personalities are noticeably altered.

12. Abusing or degrading God's creation.

13. Holding feelings of anger, hatred or jealousy towards other persons.

14. Having a life goal of wealth, comfort, and an abundance of material possessions.

This is not to say we will never be tempted to do these things, but when temptation comes our way, as it most certainly will, the Spirit of Christ will instantly rise up within us and boldly tell us that what we are about to do is not worthy of the holiness and righteousness of the Lord of our lives. He who dwells within our being and is at the controls of our conduct would be disgraced if we engaged in these activities.

If we find ourselves falling into these unworthy actions it means there are at least some areas of our old self that have not yet been crucified with Christ.

On the other hand, when Christ is truly Lord of our lives and we have experienced resurrection transformation with him, these are the fruits that will be evident in our conduct:

1. We will respond with kindness, gentleness and honesty when we are persecuted for righteousness and because we bear the name of Christ.

2. We will happily extend forgiveness to those who have offended us, knowing that we also have been forgiven much.

3. We will assist and seek justice and wholeness for the fatherless, the widows, the poor, the despised, the outcasts, the sinners, the foreigners, the homeless and the handicapped.

4. We will sacrifice ourselves to bring peace where there is conflict, to bring healing to the sick, to console the troubled, to help the disadvantaged to have justice, to shelter the homeless and feed the hungry.
5. We will willingly suffer hardship, inconvenience and deprivation in servitude to others that invites them to become reconciled to God and enjoy His salvation.
6. Our mouths, out of the goodness of our hearts, will speak words of encouragement, affirmation and blessing to all those we meet.
7. We will gladly use our God-given gifts to preserve unity in the community of Christ and to build up others in their faith and maturity in Christ.
8. Our limited goals for the acquisition of material riches will be guided by the principle that "Godliness with contentment is great gain...if we have food and clothing, with these we will be content" (1 Tim. 6: 6-8).

Those whose conduct looks like this are models of Christ. At the end-time judgment, they will hear the welcoming words of the King, "Come, you who are blessed by my Father, inherit the kingdom prepared for you from the foundation of the world" (Matt. 25:31-46).

## The power of love and God's fullness

In verses 17-19 of this passage, the reader's attention is drawn to the importance of love in the relationship of the believers with

God and with Christ. The image of 'being rooted and grounded in love illustrates our relationship with God as like that of a vigorously growing plant or tree that has its roots firmly in the nurture-giving soil of love. That life-giving relationship enables believers to understand our inclusion in the greatness of God's power, presence and purpose for the salvation of his creation. This loving intimacy of inclusion with God is something we know about, but it goes even beyond our ability to comprehend. It surpasses reason and logic that God should choose us as his people, adopting us as his sons and sharing his riches with us. Our loving relationship with God is the grounding out of which grows our faithfulness to him. It is the power of love, God's love for us and ours for him, that fills us with his righteousness. It is this love that overcomes the enmity, separation and alienation that was once between us. God's inclusive love within us goes far beyond a personal intimacy with God; it enables us to love all people and all of his creation the same way he loves.

## Doxology

The doxology is a concluding statement of blessing and worship towards God and at the same time is encouragement for the believer to trust God concerning the knowledge of God he has been hearing in the preceding instruction. In the first three chapters, the author has been informing us of the great program of victory God is executing through Messiah Jesus in bringing all things under the authority of Christ and forever banishing evil in the new heaven and new earth. But besides all that, in addition "he is able to do far more abundantly than all that we ask or think, according to the power at work within us". In other words, we are unable to verbalize or even imagine the great things God is yet going to do through His people, the community of Christ.

These are great words to read and rest in when we are discouraged and feel heavy opposition by the enemy. The doxology also prepares us for the next half of Ephesians: instructions in discipleship living.

## Pray/Read 3:14-21

Our Father, I bow in awe, seized by the wonder of your plan to bring your glorious creation back to yourself eternally through Jesus Christ. As Father, you have named every people group on earth, including my own. Because you are our Father we belong to you and receive from you all the blessings and glory that belong with your holiness and righteousness. We receive these into our innermost being through the Spirit who transforms our hearts and lives so that we are able to live as Jesus lived when he was, like us, a human. All this grows out of your unending love for us, which is unwilling to see us suffer under the power of the evil one. Finite and weak as we are, we nevertheless pray for a renewed vision of the length, the breadth the height and the depth of your love. May that consciousness empty us of ourselves so that we may be filled with your fullness to do the great work to which you have called us in union with Jesus Christ. Amen

## Reflection, Discussion, Action

1. Describe how you experience or would like to experience the indwelling Spirit of Christ in your life.

2. Describe how love is the essential quality of the believer's indwelling relationship with Christ. What is the impact on one's life when he is rooted and grounded in the love of God?

3. How can you help yourself or others experience the crucifixion of the old self, the old man within?

4. List and explain some of the ways your life has been changed or is being changed into Christ likeness.

# Lesson SEVEN

# A Community Worthy of Christ
Ephesians 4:1-16

## Lesson 7 Passage overview

Chapter 4 begins the second half of the epistle. It also marks a movement forward in the progression of the letter. Chapters 1-3 establish the lofty position of God's adopted sons and daughters in righteousness and in their seating in the heavenlies with Christ, all this very lofty, heady stuff. But this chapter begins the ethical side of the blessings of being in Christ. The last three chapters are chucked full of our responsibility to live in a manner worthy of our status in the Beloved.

The apostle's first appeal is that our life together must be a reflection of the oneness and unity of the Godhead: Father, Son and Holy Spirit. Oneness first requires four virtues on the part of every believer: humility, gentleness, patience and devotion to holding each other up in grace and love.

Second, the focus of the worship, the ministry and the devotion of the church must be on the features of oneness at the center: one body, one Spirit, one hope, one Lord, one faith, one baptism and one God and Father of us all.

Third, in verses 7-13, Christ has equipped the community of saints with gifts that minister to the body and facilitate the movement of the faithful up and into the head, Christ. This is the process of become more Christlike—in effect, our participation in the process of bringing all things under the Lordship of Christ.

In the first half of his letter the apostle clearly states his calling to make known the great mystery of God's plan for the ages and eternity: to include all peoples and all of his creation in the end-time movement of gathering up all into and under the authority of Messiah Jesus. The church, God's new covenant people, has a significant role in these momentous events. With this mission in view, the apostle notes three themes that will ensure the church's faithfulness in the performance of its mission: unity, giftedness and leadership within the community.

## Oneness in the Spirit

*Vv.1-6 I therefore, a prisoner for the Lord, urge you to walk in a manner worthy of the calling to which you have been called, with all humility and gentleness, with patience, bearing with one another in love, eager to maintain the unity of the Spirit in the bond of peace. There is one body and one Spirit—just as you were called to the one hope that belongs to your call—one Lord, one faith, one baptism, one God and Father of all, who is over all and through all and in all.*

The Trinity (Father, Son and Holy Spirit) represent a perfect oneness. They share all things of their being, their mission and their ministry in perfect, loving unity. The church, the bride of

Christ, his presence on earth, is co-opted into this divine oneness, mission and ministry. To carry out its mission within the overall plan of the Father, the church must participate in the divine unity of the Trinity.

Jesus himself anticipates this unity with his church in his own committal prayer to the Father: "Sanctify them in the truth; your word is truth. As you sent me into the world, so I have sent them into the world. And for their sake I consecrate myself, that they also may be sanctified in truth. I do not ask for these only, but also for those who will believe in me through their word, that they may all be one, just as you, Father, are in me, and I in you, that they also may be in us, so that the world may believe that you have sent me. The glory that you have given me I have given to them, that they may be one even as we are one, I in them and you in me, that they may become perfectly one, so that the world may know that you sent me and loved them even as you loved me" (John 17:17-23).

The unity Paul speaks of in Ephesians 4 has both a vertical and horizontal dimension. Vertically, we are united in oneness with the Father's vision for the salvation of his creation under the Lordship of Messiah Jesus. This oneness happens because we have seen God's glory in the life, death and resurrection of Christ, and we have responded to his call to be covenanted with him in holiness and love. The fruit of this relationship is that we are able to walk in a manner worthy of the calling. Speaking of our oneness and our relationship, Paul includes both the individual and communal relationships of our oneness.

On the horizontal dimension, 4:4-6 informs us the disciples of Jesus are united because we have "one hope...one Lord, one faith, one baptism, one God and Father of all." Paul's exhortation in Ephesians 4 is especially concerned with unity among the disciples on this horizontal level. In chapter 2 he tells us that unity among the disciples should not be a problem when we recognize that the walls of disunity in the church have been broken down, laid flat because, in his death, Jesus has made us one, killing the hostility between us.

Even with this Christological reality, Paul recognizes that some of us may still have problems with each other; therefore to the work of the Messianic peacemaker he adds some heavenly relational lubricating ointment: we will also need copious doses of "humility and gentleness, with patience, bearing with one another in love, eager to maintain the unity of the Spirit in the bond of peace" (4:3). If we can but have the humility, gentleness and patience of Christ, bearing with the flaws of the other because we love these people, and if we honestly possess an eagerness for unity of the Spirit, we should easily overcome the issues that threaten oneness. What really is the genesis, the test, for Christian unity and oneness? Paul's list of commonalities shows us the evidences for oneness with other believers:

***We follow after Jesus Christ, the Lord of the Church, in a relationship of obedience and covenanted discipleship.*** We believe Jesus, in his earthy life, becomes the norm for all of his disciples in terms of our world view and conduct.

***We have all been through the same baptism.*** Baptism in this context means that we have publicly declared that we are no longer slaves of Satan and we are now adopted Sons of God, and that we are first and foremost citizens of God's kingdom. This declaration is made in a symbolic public ceremony involving water in some form. How the water is administered and how the ceremony is conducted is not specified in scripture. The important issue is that we make this public declaration of change in allegiance out of the kingdom of darkness and into the kingdom of God.

***We worship/serve one God who is none other than the Lord God Jehovah,*** the God of Abraham, Isaac and Jacob and the Father of our Lord Jesus Christ.

***We are unconditionally committed to faith/faithfulness with this divine oneness.***

***We live in the eschatological assured hope that God's eternal plan will one day be consummated.*** In the meanwhile, with patience, "we are waiting for new heavens and a new earth in which righteousness dwells" (2 Pet. 3:13).

Therefore, I am in the universal community of Christ with anyone having those faith values and understandings, regardless of our denominational tags, doctrinal inclinations, social status, political preferences, ethnic backgrounds or any other man-made descriptors. When I meet new folks, with a little conversation I will soon discover where they are on the faith oneness scale. I am frequently amazed to find Christians with denominational identifications different from my own and from a different culture, but we are in oneness with regard to our world view, our, faith and our ethics. It soon becomes obvious whether or not we share citizenship in God's kingdom. I am likewise surprised at times how people, cut from essentially the same theological cloth as mine, are far from me on this Ephesians litmus test.

A few years ago when I was travelling across the U.S., I was with a host couple for the weekend who took me to their church on Sunday morning. The congregation's statement of faith read much like my own: the differences were minor. This particular Sunday was the first Sunday following the Fourth of July, the U.S. independence celebration. But the pastor's message that morning upset me! This church was in a profound spiritually adulterous relationship with the U.S. conservative political party. My oneness indicator with that church went way over on the negative side of the scale. We are light years apart on our understanding of Christology and ecclesiology. Oneness with other Christians has little to do with lofty theological documents, ecumenical conventicles and joint faith resolutions. Oneness is realized through our way of doing and being Christian much more than in paper-bound dogmas.

Another flawed manner of understanding oneness is to equate it with homogeneity. In the same cross-country excursion mentioned above, I had the opportunity to visit some Christian communities where members are virtually all descendents of a common Germanic gene pool; these people talk alike, look alike, dress alike, use the same cookbooks, and were easily identifiable from half a mile away. However, they suffer schisms about as regularly as Guinea Bissau has coups. You don't arrive at unity and oneness simply by all being cut from the same bolt of cultural cloth.

Christian oneness is intentionally and purposefully cross-cultural. The church of Christ is a living, visible community of culturally, socially and economically diverse people brought together in peace and love because, in his death and resurrection, Christ brought an end to the powers that divide on those bases. There are two culturally prevalent dividing walls that the church in West Africa would do well to focus on: tribalism and gender inequality. The greatest peace offering the church can bring to West African society is the melting down of tribal animosities fueled by suspicions, denigration, mistrust and ancient curses. Put that offering together with one that highly values all persons despite their gender, economic status and social rank. The result is a community of Christ inclusively gathering diverse peoples into one harmonious body under the headship of Christ, fulfilling God's mission for the church exactly.

*Vv.8-10 But grace was given to each one of us according to the measure of Christ's gift. Therefore it says, "When he ascended on high he led a host of captives, and he gave gifts to men." (In saying, "He ascended," what does it mean but that he had also descended into the lower regions, the earth? He who descended is the one who also ascended far above all the heavens, that he might fill all things.)*

## The community gifted and graced

A key phrase in v. 8 is "each one." Each one means that Christ, the giver of gifts, has bestowed on each and every member of the body grace and gifts. Grace can be understood as divine empowerment in the exercise of a particular gift. The church modeled here is not a two-tiered entity with gifted, high powered elite in the upper echelon and the spectator mass filling the pews. That is the common image of church in West Africa. In Ephesians, however, each one participating in the body has been measured gifts according to the fullness and riches of Christ, gifts that help us along the way to the oneness and mission spoken of in the previous verses. In North America, church has degenerated into a Sunday morning make-me-feel-good entertainment spectacular. The mega church with the best crowd-pleasing, choreographed show of professional actors for the Sunday morning lineup is assured of having throngs of spectators.

We are headed that same direction in West Africa. The difference is that what entertains and makes Africans feel good about themselves is significantly different from that sought after by North Americans.

The radical, New Testament patterned church, on the other hand, sees every member specially gifted by Christ to make a meaningful contribution to the oneness, completion and witness of the body. Where do these gifts come from? How do they happen? Where do I find mine?

The quote from Psalm 68:18, edited somewhat in its Ephesians 4:8 setting, is a picture of the victorious Christ leading captives taken from among the "sons of disobedience" and the "children of wrath" (see Ephesians chapter 2) and seating them with himself in the heavenlies. These captives have joined Christ because they have decided they no longer want to live by the desires of the flesh, they no longer want to be counted among Satan's slaves, and they do not want to face the consequences of being in rebellion against God. Instead, they desire to change their allegiance over to the victorious Christ; they want to be citizens, servants, slaves, captives, sons (any of those terms will work) of God's kingdom. Having made that decision, they are joined to the people of Christ and moved with him into the heavenlies. There he gives them ministry gifts so they can be actively involved in the extension of his kingdom into the darkest corners of earth. Captivity itself becomes a captive as the faithful joyfully submit to the Lordship of Christ.

Why does Christ give these new servants gifts? Prior to their conversion, their gifts or faculties (their minds, hearts, souls, spirits, wills and bodies) were all at the disposal of Satan, and he used them for his destructive purposes. But now that life under Satan is history and they have a new Lord, Messiah Jesus, he fills their minds, hearts and bodies with his fullness so that with their entire being they are able to serve the kingdom of God.

In God's scheme of things, his mystery of the ages, where the community of Christ's disciples is charged with the responsibility of demonstrating to the powers the reality of the victorious, glorified Christ, there is no room for spectators. Each participant is enlisted and gifted to combat the already defeated enemy. How should the church in West Africa be taking on the responsibility of helping the followers of Jesus to recognize, receive and use their Christ-given gifts? This is the question I put to some of my African pastor friends. They all agreed we have much to challenge us here.

Mobilizing the gifts that Christ has placed in our congregations though the lives of the believers starts with congregational leaders who have a vision for their faith community as a beachhead of God's kingdom in the urban neighborhood or village where the church meets. Leaders need to be asking how they can we facilitate the coming of God's kingdom in their neighborhoods. (This goes way beyond traditional door to door evangelism.) We need to be in conversation with our neighbors to discover what blessings God's people could bring to the neighborhood that would meet the spiritual, social, economic and health needs of the people where we live.

In the neighborhood where I live, the church has ministry through an orphanage, a medical clinic and a day care center for boys living on the streets of Ziguinchor, Senegal. During the course of a week, these ministries alone touch the lives of literally hundreds of needy persons outside God's kingdom. To that could be added the contacts and friends the church members have in their own daily round of activities, hundreds more contacts with people needing to be touched with the grace and love of God. This church deeply is immersed in ministry opportunities. God wants this community of faith to be gifted, enabling them to be the presence of Christ in the lives of hundreds of people with whom they are in regular contact through the church ministries and the daily lives of the church members. Somehow we need to do a much better job of connecting our church members with the gifts and enabling power of God so that the community of Christ is in fullness and oneness with the mission mandate of our Lord.

That brings us to our next topic:

## The gifts and the gifted

*V.11-And he gave the apostles, the prophets, the evangelists, the shepherds and teachers*

Verse 11 is something of a progressive list of people the Lord provided for the founding and the development of the church at Ephesus, harking back to 2:20 and 3:5 where Paul specifies the founding messengers of the gospel: apostles and prophets, with Christ, the cornerstone. These apostles and prophets either came to Ephesus as missionaries or were available among the early converts. The people listed in v.11 had the function of ministering the word, the message of God about Messiah Jesus who had come to establish God's new people of faith. Priscilla, Aquila and Apollos would be included in the list of early ministers in Ephesus.

They were the people fulfilling the commission by Jesus to go, make disciples and teach them to observe all that he had commanded. The purpose of the verse is simply to list the people who were active in the initial establishment of the church. It shouldn't be read as an exhaustive or exclusive list of offices or roles of church hierarchy.

With the departure or deaths of the original apostles, the first messengers, the task of proclamation was taken up by evangelists. As communities of faith grew, there became a need for teachers and shepherds. The teachers and shepherds mentioned in connection with the church of the New Testament had responsibility to teach the word, guide spiritual growth, care for the weak, give oversight to congregations and be stewards of the apostolic deposit (1 Tim. 6:20; 2 Tim. 1:14). The words teacher, pastor and shepherd are not used in the context of a proposed order of church organization into offices or positions. They are simply descriptive words of ministries performed by members of the congregation who are gifted accordingly.

In communities of faith that developed around the ministry of Christ and the first apostles, the nomenclature and stratification of offices and ministries in the communities are scant or nonexistent. People who were gifted to minister in the community became willing, humble servants to others in whatever the Lord called them to do for the extension of God's kingdom.

All that changed in the early decades of the second century when Ignatius, bishop of Antioch, promoted a rigid hierarchy of churchly offices with the bishops (of course) at the top of the heap. Orders and subjection flowed downward, obeisance and deference flowed up. Not only that, it was he who partitioned church into clergy and laity, in effect rebuilding walls that Christ had broken down.

What does this say to those of us who are keen to see a re-establishment of the radical church and return to our foundation of the apostles and prophets with Christ the chief cornerstone? What will we do with ministry gifts, ministry roles and lines of responsibility and authority? Perhaps we will need some role designations, but could they not be emptied of status, pride and celebrity? Are there ways we can serve the church without it turning into an ego trip? Can people have authority in the church and still be submissive to the brotherhood?

I once got acquainted with a man who had been sent out by his denomination as their apostle to a certain large geographic region, meaning that he was their top prelate for that region. Now, my understanding of the role of an apostle, based on the example of Jesus and Paul, goes something like this: "one anointed to proclaim good news to the poor, proclaim liberty to the captives and recovering of sight to the blind, to set at liberty those who are oppressed, and to proclaim the year of the Lord's favor." I had some interaction with their mission, and I never became aware that this apostle was doing anything even remotely resembling these tasks. He lived in a palatial house in an upscale part of town, was always well dressed and was chauffeured around in a big black Toyota SUV with shaded windows. He spent most of his time in his office or in church meetings where he was received with adulation by his adoring congregants and pastors.

If that's what apostles are like, I think we would best do without them.

Whatever happened to servants of the church like this one: "with far greater labors, far more imprisonments, with countless beatings, and often near death. Five times I received at the hands of the Jews the forty lashes less one. Three times I was beaten with rods. Once I was stoned. Three times I was shipwrecked; a night and a day I was adrift at sea on frequent journeys, in danger from rivers, danger from robbers, danger from my own people, danger from Gentiles, danger in the city, danger in the wilderness, danger at sea, danger from false brothers; in toil and hardship, through many a sleepless night, in hunger and thirst, often without food, in cold and exposure. And, apart from other things, there is the daily pressure on me of my anxiety for all the churches" (2 Cor. 11: 23-28).

Church leaders need to be back-of-the-line servants, getting their hands dirty in the work of ministering to the needs of others. In the radical church we don't need salaried, career leadership professionals. We need simple, willing servants committed to the messy work of doing God's will on earth as it is in heaven. Even if just two or three people in the congregation follow the servant model of Jesus, they will be emulated by the rest of the flock.

Being a down-in-the-dirt servant is a challenge in any culture, but it is particularly challenging in West Africa where servitude and slavery are viewed very negatively as ignoble badges of shame. By contrast, being a master with power and honor is what most Africans, especially males, aspire to arrive at. But if our goal is truly to "grow up in every way into him who is the head, into Christ," as v. 16 puts it, then servanthood should not be a problem. Jesus was the perfect model of a self-giving, life-giving servant. Why would a radical disciple of Jesus want to be anything other than like his Master?

*Vv. 12-13 building up the body of Christ, until we all attain to the unity of the faith and of the knowledge of the Son of God, to mature manhood, to the measure of the stature of the fullness of Christ*

The gifts of the Spirit are often understood as enabling some to have authority and power over others especially to enforce behavioral changes. But that is not what we find in these verses. The Spirit giftings are to assist in restoring, putting in order and healing lives that have been marred by sin. The gifts enable new believers to come into the knowledge of Jesus, to conform their lives to be like his and to transition into the fullness that Christ is recreating them to be. That is what is meant by building up the body of Christ and arriving at the stature of the fullness of Christ.

The situation we generally see in West African churches is that we have many people who have almost no knowledge of

Jesus, the very cornerstone and bridegroom of the church. The only thing they can tell you about Jesus is that he died on the cross to save them from their sins so that they get to go to heaven when they die. Perhaps these also believe that if one prays hard enough and long enough Jesus can even perform a miracle for them like helping them get a visa to America. Period. People who have that much knowledge of Jesus are like the wheat that was sown among the weeds. It can start to grow just a little bit, but it is soon choked out by the competing weeds and they lose their spiritual relationship with Jesus (Matt. 13).

## You can do it

What we lack in our churches are people, just humble, radical, sacrificial servants of Jesus, who will come alongside new believers and seekers, walking step by step with them as they come into full knowledge and faithfulness to Jesus. If someone (like you!) will do that for them, they also be well prepared to do the work of ministry themselves, helping their friends also to come into the measure of the fullness of Christ.

The responsibility for nurturing each other is laid on every Christian. Ministering to others in the body of Christ doesn't wait for a special appointment to a specific role in the church such as pastor, teacher or evangelist. It is true that some are more mature in their faith and experience as a Christian and have a more developed understanding of the Word; still, even new believers may be winsome evangelists and a refreshing wind of grace for all of us.

The highly developed, rigid hierarchy of roles and appointments we see in many churches actually becomes a roadblock to the release of the Spirit for everyone to share the work of building each other up, the very purpose for which the gifts were originally given.

Why is God calling you to this ministry? He needs you because the pastor can't do it—he's too busy trying to perform miracles and hassling people about giving their tithes and offerings. The Apostle can't do it—he's too busy entertaining other church dignitaries and tending to the pomp of his position. The Bible teacher can't do it—he's too busy trying to organize his systematic theology. The missionary can't do it—he's too busy trying to leap the cultural obstacles. Besides, too many people in these appointed, sanctified roles are on such an ego trip they are severely handicapped in their attempts to effect spiritual growth and change in immature believers, treating them with contempt, ordering them to grow up and making intimidated puppets out of them.

But you can do it. Just go back to the first two lessons in this study guide where Paul talks about all the unsearchable riches of Christ, the attributes and mission of Christ, and begin to share with your seeker friends the wonder and the glory of Christ and all the ways he wants to transform their lives into being like him. Once you finish what you find in Ephesians 1, continue teaching your disciple friend by going to the Gospel of Matthew and walk through the life of Christ, teaching him about what it means to become a disciple of Jesus and to come to mature manhood in Christ.

In your ministry to Jesus-seekers, you are able to do far more than just preach to them. You are able to model for them what it means to be a new creation in Christ. In your actions, attitudes and spirit they will see the compassion, forgiveness, mercy and gentleness of Jesus himself. In fact, they will probably learn more about Jesus by observing your actions and attitudes than by all the right teaching you are giving to them. Relating to new believers and seekers of Jesus in this way will build them into the love and the fullness of Christ.

You won't be given a title for this work, you won't receive a salary and your friends may not even know you are busy doing this ministry. But Jesus knows, the Holy Spirit knows, and they are there to empower and gift you to do the work they have called you to in the body of Christ!

## Reflection, discussion, action

1. Read John chapter 17 two or three times, allowing the words and desires of Jesus to deeply penetrate your heart. Allow yourself to be drawn into the oneness that Jesus shares with the Father. Pray with Jesus that the last thought of the chapter (v.26) will become more and more a reality for you: "that the love with which you have loved me may be in them, and I in them."

2. Talk about times when you have met Christians from other cultures and other churches and how you have discovered your shared relationship with Jesus.

3. Think about and talk about ways your life intersects with unbelievers and how you have begun to share with them your hope in Christ. Not that you preach to them, but that you become a servant to them in a way that encourages their openness to Christ. How are you able to minister the love of Christ into the brokenness of their lives?

4. Discuss with others in your faith community opportunities your community has to bring hope and transformation to your village or neighborhood. What is a plan of action that might inaugurate this ministry?

# Lesson EIGHT

## Two Men: One Old, One New
## Two Paths: One to Death. One to Life
Ephesians 4:17- 5:2

**Lesson 8 Passage overview**

In these 13 verses the apostle leaves little room for doubt or ambiguity about the traits of the new man in Christ versus the old man controlled by Satan. The fact that he is so specific and black and white makes one wonder what the situation was in the Ephesian churches. Were there actually people in the churches who were giving themselves to every unclean work, using rotten language with each other and alienated from the life in God? Or is he just talking about their former life before their adoption into God's family?

The qualities of the new man in Christ are impressive:

- A renewed mind after that of God
- Behavior imitating that of God
- Following the model of Christ by laying down our lives to help others into Christ
- Assured that they are the forgiven, loved children of God
- Life-long learners of the ways, wisdom and will of God
- Walking in the truth and the good
- Taking responsibility for themselves and others by working with their hands

- Communicating truthfully and graciously
- Kind, compassionate and forgiving

In a neighborhood where I once lived, every morning about six o'clock one could hear loud singing and praying going on several houses away. The couple in this house were actively involved in church and made no attempt to hide their Christian faith. They frequently confronted people about their spiritual condition and urged them to "let Jesus into their hearts." The woman was a worship leader and did a respectable job at it. The man was particularly good at directing conversation into spiritual issues, even when he was talking to total strangers. In time, however, it became more and more evident that this religiosity was all a façade. They were secretly involved in witchcraft, they helped themselves to other people's property, they seldom spoke the unvarnished truth, they were savage slanderers and they eventually abandoned their children and each other. They found new mates and started families with them. Everything in their lives literally fell apart. Their elaborate façade of Christianity was reduced to a heap of rubble.

When I consider this couple and many others who are on that same track, I ponder why people would even want to go through all the bother of giving the appearance of good or godliness when they know, and soon the whole world will know, that their lives are a sham. And even if they were able to continue the charade, God would know, and they would sooner or later be faced with judgment and loss. In Ephesians 4, there is little doubt that the same problem persisted in the churches the apostle Paul was writing to centuries ago, only decades after the birth of the Church.

In v.1, he urges them to walk in a manner worthy of Christ; apparently there were those who were walking in a manner unworthy.

In v.14, he warns them about being giddy, dolts carried about by every wind of deceit and craftiness; apparently there were those among them who thrived on deceit.

In vv 17, he describes people who live like the pagans, in ignorance, hard-hearted, greedy, false and impure; apparently there were people in the Christian community still living after the desires of the flesh.

We can come to some resolution about the problem of people wanting to have it both ways when we look at the example of our first parents in Genesis 3. Here Satan, the great deceiver, actually convinces them that they can have it both ways: they can be like God with all his wisdom, power and discernment and at the same time live on a second track of disobedience to God. The temptation to duplicity and pretense has been a companion of mankind from the beginning of time and it is still with us big time, even in the church of West Africa. We are easily deceived into thinking that we can enjoy all the benefits of God and godliness and at the same time be serving the fallenness of our flesh. Many even use godliness, piety and Christian profession as a foil for advancing personal greed and all types of fleshly desires.

How do we deal with this deceitful inclination even in the church? That's the question the apostle is addressing in Ephesians 4. With the patience and love of an apostolic father to the Ephesian believers, he instructs them to put off (that is, to remove from their hearts and lives the power of the old man) and to put on the new man, in their hearts, their minds and their conduct through the transforming grace of God.

Why do people attempt to play games with God's holiness and continue to live according to the flesh? It is because "they are darkened in their understanding, alienated from the life of God because of the ignorance that is in them, due to their hardness of heart. They have become callous and have given themselves up to sensuality, greedy to practice every kind of impurity. (4:18-19). In other words, it is not just out of a sheer inability to know or to reason; it is because they are deliberately attempting to live both ways. As a result, God has given them up to the concrete-hard determination of their corrupted hearts to live in disobedience to his will. "'Given themselves up to" sensuality, greed and impurity recognizes they have willfully and openly chosen to be disobedient. Take special note of the word greedy. These people have an insatiable desire, not just in terms of sexual lust, but they are greedy to practice all kinds of actions that are contrary to God's design for life, including economic and material excesses. Those are stern words of warning for us today. Please note in these verses how Paul attempts to create distance between their former and present style of living. When we understand the ugliness of sin compared to the beauty, order, peace and joy of life in Christ, it builds within us a natural resistance to that which is impure and fallen.

I have frequently heard the testimonies of people who have come out of the horrors of the animistic, demonic lifestyle and how they now enjoy the goodness of God and the love of the community of Christ; there is no way they have any desire to return to the former. When I hear those testimonies coming out of both a changed heart and the new way of walking in Christ, I know their conversion and new relationship with God are for real.

When people use all the right God-talk words, but their actions, attitudes and life goals are self-pleasing and of the flesh, then their faith is obvious only a charade.

*Vv. 20-24 But that is not the way you learned Christ!—-assuming that you have heard about him and were taught in him, as the truth is in Jesus, to put off your old self, which belongs to your former manner of life and is corrupt through deceitful desires, and to be renewed in the spirit of your minds, and to put on the new self, created after the likeness of God in true righteousness and holiness.*

Paul doesn't let the message rest at the negative, accusatory point; he moves on in vv. 20-24 to help the readers understand what it means to learn Christ and put on the new self. Learning Christ goes far beyond learning about him or even memorizing his sayings. The biblical message is not just learning about God; it is receiving a divine person into our total being. It is about giving up our own will and replacing it with his will in the person and Spirit of Christ. Learning, in the way Paul expresses it here, goes far beyond acquiring right doctrine, dogma or a system of theology.

In this intimate relationship with Christ, we encounter him and are formed and discipled by him in a bonded relationship, all in the context of the community of faith. We learn to live by the fruit of this relationship with Christ. Perhaps one of the key issues we learn of Christ is about his faithfulness and submission to the will and purposes of his Father. Another would be to learn of and participate in the depth of the Father-Son's love relationship.

As we learn of Christ in this way, falling back into the old, pagan, self-dominated way of living becomes less and less of an option. The transformation from the old to the new self is clearly a process of coming into the fullness of God. It is neither a once-and-done, external, up-in-heaven transaction (as in some evangelical thought) nor an overnight, suddenly black to white event. And it takes a good deal more than raising one's hand at a gospel invitation and repeating the sinner's prayer.

The last seven verses of chapter 4 have the appearance of random instructions about Christian behavior on how to control our anger, use our tongues and our hands. I am going to be offering a slightly alternate understanding and one that fits better with the theme of the passage: putting off the old and putting on the new.

## Speaking the truth v. 25

Verse 25 is likely more than a command simply to stop lying and start telling the truth, even though that in itself is a worthy suggestion. The verse can also be rendered as "put off THE LIE" as a parallel to putting off the old man in verse 22. The LIE is another way of noting the old manner of living according to deception and falseness of man in rebellion against the God of truth. Although it isn't noted as such, Paul could have gleaned this thought from the prophet Zechariah 8:16-17: "These are the things that you shall do: Speak the truth to one another; render in your gates judgments that are true and make for peace; do not devise evil in your hearts against one another, and love no false oath, for all these things I hate, declares the Lord." Deceiving ourselves and those around us is typical of a people who are openly in rebellion, from the heart, against God. As Zechariah notes, untruth is the stuff of an unjust and conflictive social order.

It is of interest that Paul directs the injunction for truthfulness at people in the church! Do believers need to be ordered to stop living by the lies and deceit of human cunningness and craftiness of deceitful schemes (4:14)? Apparently so, and apparently it is the case when we have active church members living under the deceit of Satan and somehow thinking they can get away with putting truth together with lies.

When persons in the body are living the lie, it is imperative that the church community speak, in love, directly and unequivocally to that brother or sister about the error. I am aware that speaking correction in African society is many times unacceptable because one does not reproach someone older and of a higher status than himself. Thus, it isn't easy for a 23-year-old, well aware of the duplicity in the life of his pastor 15 years his senior, to offer correction to this leader. If he is not able to do that, then someone else or some group in the church needs to do it because, as Paul says, we are all members together of this body and we have this obligation to the body. And the body of Christ is required to witness truth to the powers, even if that power has invaded the church.

## Being angry (provoked) about sin vv.26-27

I have been in numerous discussions on verses 26 and 27, concerning the appropriateness or inappropriateness of anger on the part of the Christian. An alternate understanding of these verses is to let the imperative "Be angry" stand. In other words, go ahead; get angry about things that represent the power of evil in the church and the larger society. Get passionate about injustice, poverty, and marginalization of people of color, the despoliation of the environment and the abuse of power in government or the church.

I live near a small village about eight km. (five miles) outside the city of Ziguinchor, Senegal. Everyday there is a parade of trucks and trailers hauling garbage and sewage from the city and dumping it on landfills near our village. It is our village elders who have given permission for this environmental catastrophe, and it is their pockets that are being lined by the city for this easy way of getting rid of their garbage. The landfill is constantly burning with clouds of acrid, poisonous smoke filling the air we must breathe. We are angry about this and rightly so. We need to be angry with this ruination of God's good earth, the home for the many creatures to whom He granted this beautiful area. Unfortunately, His creation is being endangered because of the greed and injustice of a few people who benefit from living the lie. So, many people of the neighborhood are joining together to demand rectification of this evil.

This is a good example of why God's people need to be angry and provoked when His will and righteousness are being ignored. Not letting the sun go down on our wrath means that we are vigorously and persistently speaking the truth and calling for God's justice and will to be honored in our community.

However, in our provocation and passion we must not allow our spirits and emotions to move us to the point of hostility towards the offenders. Grievous though their sin may be, they must ever be within the scope of love, mercy and the hope for their redemption. When we start referring to the sons of disobedience as the accursed, the reprobate, vile and unclean, we have gone too far. Although they may be all of the above, that is not our judgment call to make; let's leave the judgment and condemnation to God Almighty. He will render perfect justice on the rebellious. Our task is to be channels and facilitators of God's light, mercy and new creation for those alienated from him.

At times we may find it necessary to be provoked even at irregularities within the community of Christ. In the radical community of Christ, it is a very serious offense for a member to live in a way that brings dishonor and shame to the glory and holiness of God represented in the life of the community of Christ. Moreover, we have a serious commitment to our family in Christ, mutually helping each other to grow up into Christ our head. Sin in the body needs to be dealt with in and by the body, but done in a manner that seeks, first and foremost, the reconciliation and restoration to the offender. Jesus left us with instructions on how loving, restorative correction is carried out by the church. (Matt. 18: 15-20). Using this model, we have a precise pattern for becoming angry and at the same time not sinning.

## Hands that help; words that bless vv.28-29

Verses 28 and 29 offer two examples of the contrast between the old sinful nature and the re-created self under the Lordship of Christ.

A thief, who has been transformed by Christ, will use his hands to do creative labor, enabling him to help those in need. The unbeliever's hands look out only for his own needs. He will take from others in need, appropriating for himself what the needy rightfully deserve. The hands of the new person in Christ, views his hands as an asset, a tool, in the sharing of God's goodness, especially to the poor, the disadvantaged and needy (v28).

In West Africa we see multitudes of young men with their arms folded, idly lounging about, spending most of the day socializing with their buddies. Can you imagine the transformation one would see in Africa if all those idle hands and minds could be mobilized to develop and bless this continent? This continent has the potential of being transformed into something close to the Garden of Eden if suddenly millions of youth would decide to be Christlike.

In the many years I have spent in Africa, I have witnessed a good number of new-man transformations on the part of African youth. An evidence of authentic transformation is that their hands quickly become very busy and industrious as they work to bring a better standard of living to their families and communities. This transformation is a joy and blessing to behold!

Transformed speech is another significant area of concern for African faith communities. Back in the first days of my arrival in West Africa, I worked side by side with Africans on the Mercy Ship, Anastasis. One of my first cultural shocks was to listen to the brutal speech Africans use on each other. I was mortified at what I was hearing. Africans absolutely delight in pulverizing the spirit and character of others, especially if their target is beneath them in age and social standing. But I did take note that within minutes after such a verbal assault, the challengers were soon again jovial friends.

In this culture there is somehow a need to establish a pecking order, frequently accomplished through intimidating speech. However, believers who have their relationship with God in order no longer need to be concerned about the social pecking order; they, like Jesus, are back of the line servants ready to give themselves to others in both speech and actions. As a new person in Christ the goal of our talking should be to "give grace to those who hear" (v. 29). Our words should be such that help others to experience God's power that transforms persons into the likeness of Jesus. Thus, we speak words of blessing, peace and encouragement to everyone.

What's puzzling to me is that I know from firsthand experience that Africans are quite capable of this kind of speech because that is the way Africans almost always address me. I am blessed over and over by the kind, encouraging, affirming words of my African friends. It's one of the reasons I so much enjoy being among them. I am puzzled they can talk to an elderly Western missionary so graciously, why don't they do the same for each other? They would be amazed at the power of words of blessing, power to facilitate change and Christlikeness in the hearers. They would be pleased with the results!

## Maintain the companionship of the Holy Spirit v.30

This single verse exhortation is grounded in the understanding that maintenance of oneself and the community of faith as a new creation in Christ depends on the empowering presence of the Holy Spirit of Christ. Therefore, we are admonished not to take actions or use speech in a way that impedes the Spirit's enablement among us. We are not to be presumptuous about the "'sealing (by the Spirit) for the day of redemption."As believers whose lives and spirits are in Christ, we have the assurance that God's Spirit will keep us blameless for the inevitable approaching judgment day. We must not be arrogant or superficial about the promise of the Spirit. The Spirit assures us of his keeping power, but it is premised on our ongoing faithfulness. The letter to the Ephesians provides a catalog of the power and work of the Holy Spirit in the lives of the believer and among the community of faith: The Spirit is a keeping, assuring presence as we look forward to eternity (1:13-14).

We are brought near to God and have access to him through the Spirit (2:18, 22).

He strengthens us in our deep, inner being so that Christ dwells there (3:16-17).

The Spirit enables unity in the body (4:3).

His presence enables our worship times with purposeful musical expressions (5:18-19).

Therefore, in our daily walk as disciples of Christ, we need to say "no" to actions, words and attitudes that would spoil the image of Christ being created within and among us. The Spirit provides the discernment and direction we need to walk in the footsteps of the Master we follow.

## The way of loving relationships- vv 31-32

Here we are again, back at the topic of anger. This is anger in the sense we more typically think of it. Anger here is a hateful, destructive passion that destroys relationships and abandons faithfulness and oneness. The command to be angry in v.26 is anger provoked because God's righteousness is dishonored, and correction in love is meant to bring behavior back in line with expectations of people living in the new self. The anger in v.31, on the other hand, is emotional passion that develops out of bitterness and jealousy. Its evidences are argumentation, interpersonal conflicts and evil speaking. This is the kind of anger that needs to be put away from the community. In place of destructive anger, people of the new life will imitate the character of their Father (v.32). He is kind, tenderhearted and forgiving towards those who are offensive. The character of the Father is good, gracious, generous and pardoning towards the children so dear to him, even if they are out of order. Those qualities need to be abundantly evident in ongoing relationships and routine interactions among the saints.

## Imitate God; be as Christ- 5: 1-2

The command here to be imitators of God recalls the corrupted offer of the deceiver in Gen. 3:5 where Adam and Eve are offered the chance to seize and subvert the power of God for their own benefit. The fake proposal of Satan would supposedly have made Adam and Eve like God in that they would be empowered to serve themselves and control their own world and destiny. Satan has never stopped laying that bogus offer out before mankind.

In Ephesians, believers are encouraged to find the true basis for sharing in the glory and power of God as his adopted, beloved children. This authentic being like God comes as the community participates in the extension of God's will, his glory, his kingdom and his salvation to the world in which we live. A beautiful summary of what it means to be like God is provided for us in 2 Peter 1:3-4, "His divine power has granted to us all things that pertain to life and godliness, through the knowledge of him who called us to his own glory and excellence, by which he has granted to us his precious and very great promises, so that through them you may become partakers of the divine nature, having escaped from the corruption that is in the world because of sinful desire." As humans, we definitely do not become divine, but as his adopted sons, we do get to share a measure of our Father's divine nature!

This calls for discernment on the part of the community. Are leaders truly building up and equipping the community to do God's work and will, or are we seeing a Hollywood show version of Christianity in which the community is used by the leader to build his own kingdom, power and wealth? Carnally-motivated leaders have given themselves up to sensuality, pride and greed (4:19). Imitators of our Father God and Jesus Christ give themselves up to suffering, sacrifice and righteousness in their work of extending God's kingdom and equipping believers to grow up into the fullness of Christ.

True worship (v.2) is to walk in love, loving others as Christ loved, giving ourselves as a living sacrifice our worship offering to God.

## Reflection, discussion, action

1. Discuss what motivates people to live a lie. Why do you think people attempt to live on two tracks: for self and for God? What are the signs that people are not sincerely following Jesus?

2. Think about, and maybe share some of the ways, in your former life or as an immature Christian, you lived in ignorance about what God expects of His people. How did you move from ignorance into faithfulness in that part of your life?

3. Share an example of how you are provoked at the unrighteousness in either yourself or others. How are you being provoked or angered into dealing with this unrighteousness in a loving way that helps others to find God's way?

4. Talk about why it is difficult culturally for Africans to speak words of blessing and encouragement to each other.

# Lesson NINE

# Indicators of New Life in Christ
Ephesians 5: 3-21

## Lesson 9 Passage overview

This passage continues the contrast between light and darkness, but it adds the transformative, exposing dimension to the saint's lifestyle. It recalls the words of Jesus when he talked about disciples as those with a prophetic role bringing salt, light and righteousness into their cultural setting offering, an opportunity for others to know the goodness and righteousness of God.

Saints have exceptional opportunities for witness to our cultures in the areas of sexual sin, greed, evil talk and vile behavior. We walk in many ways that are totally contrary to the values and norms of our world. We should make good use of the time to expose the futility of decadent conduct and to be examples of how God has designed us to live in a manner that honors his holiness.

This witness comes in the context of being filled with God's Holy Spirit, singing, giving thanks and in being submissive and honoring to the body of believers. Our witness offers the opportunity for others to experience the transforming power of God as he brings all things under Christ's authority.

A key objective of Ephesians is to help believers know what it means to be growing into Christ, walking with Christ and participating in the reign of God in his project of bringing all things under the authority of Christ. In these verses the primary indicator of being on the right path with God is how, in our sexuality, we honor the holiness of God. How we express the God given gift of sexuality is a leading signal of which kingdom we belong to.

*Vv.3-8 But sexual immorality and all impurity or covetousness must not even be named among you, as is proper among saints. Let there be no filthiness nor foolish talk nor crude joking, which are out of place, but instead let there be thanksgiving. For you may be sure of this, that everyone who is sexually immoral or impure, or who is covetous (that is, an idolater), has no inheritance in the kingdom of Christ and God. Let no one deceive you with empty words, for because of these things the wrath of God comes upon the sons of disobedience. Therefore do not become partners with them; for at one time you were darkness, but now you are light in the Lord.*

## A Christian view of sexuality based on scripture

Paraphrasing v. 3 into a positive statement produces this: Sexual morality and purity should be the norm among you; saints should be known for their sexual propriety. In other words, our sexuality is a beautiful gift from God, a beautiful and satisfying part of how he has made us, provided it is used in the way and for the purposes of his design.

Gone are the days when sex was considered unclean and evil in itself, a function of our lower natures. Even in ancient pre-

Christian times, many cultures viewed sex solely as a means of procreation or as an activity for licentiousness, debauchery and pagan cultic worship.

An alternate understanding of sexuality came into the church following the declaration of the Roman emperor, Constantine, in 325 AD, when he made Christianity the official religion of the Roman Empire. All citizens were required to be baptized as Christians even though they remained unconverted and freely lived an ungodly life. A two-tiered Christianity, accommodating the unconverted in the church, elevated celibacy and monasticism as the model for the most devout Christians. An essentially non-sexual life was expected of church leaders and those dedicated to the service of God. But for the common Christian, sex was still viewed as a degrading, but natural, carnal evil.

Today, most Christians affirm that sexuality is a good and beautiful gift of God, a gift that gives us identity and personhood as either male or female. We are all human, but God has chosen to give us bodies, wills and emotions that vary significantly between the genders. He made us so we need each other, and in many aspects of our personhood we can be together in a complementary, wholistic sense. We believe it is right to feel positive about our bodies and our sexuality because we are created in God's image. Sexual needs and drives are a real part of our lives that cannot be ignored or obliterated. Concerning sex and marriage, faithful Christians believe and practice that sexual relations are reserved for a man and a woman united in a life-long marriage covenant. It is our understanding that this biblical teaching precludes pre-marital, extramarital, and homosexual genital activity.

I was surprised to learn that in West Africa most tribal groups, up until two or three generations ago, also forbade sexual relations outside of marriage. These had been tribal mores even before the introduction of Christianity. But today, that is all history to the point where most young women become pregnant or have a baby before marriage. Sexual promiscuity is rampant among youth; all night dances are essentially opportunities for sexual encounters, and married men have girlfriends in various communities.

The radical, obedient community of Christ presents a major challenge to this culturally accepted behavior both here in West Africa and around the world. Our message needs to be as stated above, that sexual relations are reserved for one man and one woman united in a life-long marriage covenant. This behavioral standard is expected of all persons who have publically acknowledged faithfulness to Christ and united with the church whether or not they are in church leadership. Faithfulness to one's marriage companion is of highest importance because this human relationship mirrors the relationship of Christ to his followers, the church. He is always faithful, true, respectful, just and transparent with us who claim him as Lord. Because of the parallels between husband and wife in the marriage covenant with that between Christ and the church, a blemish in the marriage covenant will also call into question faithfulness in our relationship with Christ and bring dishonor to the church.

In our Ephesians text, there is no room for misunderstanding: sexual sin belongs to lives that are totally alienated from God; persons living in this lifestyle have zero hope for any part in God's kingdom, now or eternally. Sexual relations outside of marriage defile the holiness of God and his people who are his temple.

Moving one step beyond impure sexual acts, our Ephesians text prohibits even speaking about sexual impurity in a ribald, joking or light manner. Sexual sin in our society has become (and probably always was) the stuff of entertainment. We must not even touch those secondary defilements. Sexually explicit or double entendre jokes and pornography have no place in the life of the disciple of Jesus. Why? Because sexuality belongs to God's holy and beautiful creation. Making it into an obscenity is an attempted despoliation of God's holiness and has no place in the life of the Christian. Instead of obscene words, there should be *thanksgiving*, that is worship, praising God for the way he has made things right and good. Bless Him because he has called us out of darkness and given us a place in the heavenlies, setting us free from the power of the evil one and enabling us to be living, visible examples of his righteousness.

## The evangelism of walking in the Light vv. 7-16

We have seen in this discussion of sexuality that Christians have a vastly different understanding of the meaning, value and practice in this one particular aspect of life, compared to how the sons of disobedience see and do things. The Christian understanding of sexuality and marriage is but one example of how, when the light of God's truth is boldly shining, it transforms human relations and conduct into a living example of God's intention for all of his creation. This is the witness of the church to the powers and principalities of the victory and supremacy of the resurrected Christ over evil. And it is all made plainly evident to them because of the way Christians, the children of light, conduct themselves, having been recreated into God's will for mankind.

Now, take that same principle of God's exposing light on any other aspect of life (social relationships, care of the creation, economic development, civil society and any other of life's compartments) and we have a rounded picture of the purpose and mission of God's community as we live in and among the darkness of this present age. We are not being called out of the world in the sense of separating and isolating ourselves into impenetrable enclaves of righteousness. To the contrary, we are called to walk as children of light with and among those living in darkness because it is with the fruit of light that people in darkness can find all that is good and right and true.

We do not become partners with the darkness; we take no part in the unfruitful works of darkness, but instead expose them. The exposing of what is good in contrast to what is evil doesn't happen as we wage some kind of high profile, high voltage campaign. It becomes evident in our daily walk, our conduct, the loving way we relate to each other both inside and outside the community, our honesty, our integrity, our labor, our discipline, our sense of justice, our mercy, our peacefulness, our willingness to forgive and many more qualities of life lived after the model of Jesus.

I come from a faith community that at times has gone overboard on the issue of separation from the world, attempting to establish high walls around an enclave of righteousness. The high walls make it well-nigh impossible for the seeker to be accepted into the community at the start of his faith journey. In addition, the high walls begin to create ethnic tags that go beyond a purely Christlike identity. But despite efforts at isolation, God has still been able to use those communities to demonstrate to the world the salvation, peace and wholeness God desires for all his creation.

When Christians walk in the light, even when we don't intentionally take the light to others and it is unlikely they will join us, they may come to us asking questions and observing the way we live in the peace and wholeness of God. The better intention of God for his people is that they live in their culture, freely interacting with unbelievers so that his light penetrates the darkness, providing the opportunity for transformation of the darkness. The light of God may at times result in inciting the hostility of the darkness but God does not want us to instigate hostility against the darkness or approach our unbelieving neighbors from a spirit of superiority and judgment. We come into the darkness, just as Jesus did, as a servant of God's mission, motivated by incarnating the love of God for his creation and offering the possibility of his salvation.

Here are some practical examples of how the Christian community will not walk in the darkness like the world around us, but be lights shining into the darkness of the world, transforming the dark things into light:

1. We will shine the peace of God into conflict situations.
2. We will not partner with the darkness in war and any form of violence.
3. We will bring the light of dignity and justice to the poor and marginalized.
4. We will speak words that encourage purity of thoughts and the beauty of sexuality.
5. We will not dress in ways that provoke lust and draw attention to our sexuality.

6. We will not be dominated by consumerism, insatiably greedy for more material things.
7. We will not get drunk with wine.
8. We will not partner with the world in deceit and corruption for financial gain.
9. We will not be like the world in attempting to dominate and control others.
10. We will be willing servants, always ready to demonstrate God's love to those around us.

We have spent much time and effort to develop evangelism strategies, but the best strategy for sharing the gospel is stated simply in vv. 15-17: Look carefully then how you walk, not as unwise but as wise, making the best use of the time, because the days are evil. Therefore do not be foolish, but understand what the will of the Lord is.

Just walking daily in the light of God, living a life that has been totally transformed into the image of Christ, doing the things of God and having the mind of Christ is the best evangelism strategy available to us. Yes, there needs to be oral proclamation of the gospel, but first and foremost the world wants to see the light of God in the lives, actions and attitudes of those who preach Christ.

The problem in many churches is that they are so compromised by the world, so dominated by the darkness, that they are unable to shed much light on anything. It is difficult to witness against darkness when we ourselves are heavily dominated by the darkness.

## Indicators of New Life in Christ

Here are a few examples:

1. In a church where several of the families have family members in the military you won't hear much preaching and teaching against the evil of violence, war and killing.
2. In a church where half the members are into witchcraft and consult marabous you won't hear much teaching against sorcery and the occult.
3. In a church where most of the ladies come on Sunday morning in lavish, pricey costumes with their breasts mostly exposed, you aren't going to hear many messages on modesty of attire. And you won't see many poor ladies coming to that church because their clothing is virtually only rags compared to the other women.
4. In a church where the men are attired in sharply tailored suits, shiny shoes and gold cuff links, you probably won't hear many messages from James 2:1-7.
5. In a church where the pastor and other leaders have incomes maybe three or four times that of the national average, you aren't going to hear many messages from Luke 6:20, "Blessed are you poor, for yours is the kingdom of heaven."
6. In a church where most families have TV and spend countless hours watching tawdry Mexican romance operas, you won't hear many messages about wisely redeeming the time.

Is that enough to demonstrate how walking in partnership with darkness tends to dim the light of our gospel witness and even eventually extinguish it? Does that help us to understand the significance of the message of Ephesians 5:7-14 "Therefore do not become partners with them; for at one time you were darkness, but now you are light in the Lord. Walk as children of light(for the fruit of light is found in all that is good and right and true),and try to discern what is pleasing to the Lord. Take no part in the unfruitful works of darkness, but instead expose them. For it is shameful even to speak of the things that they do in secret. But when anything is exposed by the light, it becomes visible, for anything that becomes visible is light."

Walking in the light and being lights amongst the darkness of the world is something we become stronger in, the longer we are in Christ and the closer we come into his image. Being children of the light is the normal progressive quality of the Christian pilgrimage. As we awaken, rise from the dead, begin to walk in the light and mature in Christ, we become increasingly faithful to his desires for us, and the light, in which we walk, exposes and transforms the darkness around us. This is the model and goal the apostle is holding up to the communities of Christ. The model is reflected in the v. 14 quote of a few lines from a baptismal hymn of the first century, 'Awake, O sleeper, and arise from the dead, and Christ will shine on you" (5:14).

On the contrary, if spiritually our movement is away from God and we are gradually being overcome by the surrounding darkness, the distinction between those in Christ and the sons of disobedience becomes less and less evident. This downward, regressive trend, if unchecked, continues until eventually the light of Christ is completely extinguished and we no longer possess enough light to expose any darkness.

## The walk of the wise vv. 5:15-17

In these verses, the author offers three contrasting ways of walking the way of light versus the way of darkness. The Christian walk (that is his manner of conduct) is wise, Spirit filled, redeeming the shortness of time, and it understands the will and eternal plan of God. The unwise walk, by contrast, is a walk of fools; they are careless and greedy for evil, passing their time in drunkenness and dissipation.

Verse 10 above tells us the Christian walk is one that discerns what is pleasing to the Lord. It is a walk in true wisdom. Wise disciples are those who have truly learned Christ (4:20), and they are fully connected to the mystery and plan of God for time and eternity as expressed in 1:9-¬10, 17-18 and 3:8-9. The wise are full participants in God's mission of gathering up all things in Christ and making known God's multi-varied wisdom to the powers.

The wise make use of every available opportunity of making known the will of God and exposing the darkness to the light of God's righteousness. The wise have about them a sense of urgency, knowing that time is short, that judgment and culmination are directly ahead and there is much darkness yet to be exposed to the light in these days remaining before the consummation of history.

## Filled with God's Spirit vv. 5: 18-21

A few decades ago, during the 1970s and '80s, the high-water mark of the so-called charismatic renewal, these concluding verses in chapter 5 were among the most often quoted verses of the Bible. They were mostly cited as random instructions about ecstatic worship and evidences or signs of individuals and groups who were most certainly baptized and filled with the Holy Spirit. During renewal meetings there was much pressure exerted on individuals to perform in a certain prescribed manner, emotionally and vocally, as indisputable evidence that they now had been baptized in/with the Holy Spirit. Mission accomplished!

Somehow, I just wasn't wired for that kind of ecstatic, demonstrative version of Christianity. One dear brother and his wife with whom I served in church eldership were quite worried because I wasn't showing any of the expected signs and therefore questioned if I had any connection with the Holy Spirit.

A better way of understanding these instructive verses is to view them flowing out of the context of chapter 5 in which real believers are those who have been seized by God's wisdom and his plan for bringing all things under the Lordship of Christ, and such believers are participating in God's mission by bringing his transforming light into the kingdom of darkness, reclaiming it for the kingdom of God.

As faithful believers come up against the powers of darkness, we need a steady in-filling, building up and empowering by the Holy Spirit to carry out God's assigned task for the church. Thus we regularly meet together for times of worship, *"addressing one another in psalms and hymns and spiritual songs, singing and making melody to the Lord with your heart, giving thanks always and for everything to God the Father in the name of our Lord Jesus Christ"* (vv. 19-20). The word "addressing" or in some versions "speaking" is the Greek *laleo*, a verb meaning to communicate God's wisdom and truth to the gathered congregation with the goal of edifying and building up the faith. Nothing in these verses suggests ecstatic speech or tongues.

## Subordination to exaltation: God's modus operandi

The final admonition concerning being filled with the Spirit (v.21) is the disposition of believers to be submitted to each other in the body, out of, or because of, our reverence (or fear) of Christ. Submitted means to place oneself under the other. Putting others before self is relatively common in the New Testament as the model for relating to others. That is because of the model of Christ who willingly and voluntarily submitted himself to the Father and to mankind as a way of fulfilling his own God-ordained role as Savior and Sovereign. It is through the servanthood of Jesus that God is carrying forward His eternal plan of salvation for his creation. Christ expressed his Lordship through servanthood, culminating in his death, resurrection and ultimate exaltation. This becomes the model for his followers. One is enabled and empowered to be a submitted servant through the filling of the Holy Spirit. Because we understand the significance of the submissiveness model, it makes us fear, honor and respect Christ for his position as the ultimate and sovereign judge. Since submissiveness was his road to exaltation, it is ours as well.

A few additional notes for the sake of clarity: submissiveness to each other in the church and in other social relationships dealt with in Ephesians does not mean that I must become a mindless robot, following every order that is barked out at me. It does not mean denigrating servility. It does not mean that I must be submitted to one particular individual in the body. It means I willingly submit to the expectations, advice and collective counsel of the brotherhood because they, in turn, are corporately are under the headship of Christ.

Submissiveness to each other in the body of Christ means that we are committed to the oneness of being in Christ and doing the will of Christ, understood and actualized by the church. As the church is filled with the Spirit and is submitted to the headship of Christ, it should not be a problem for me to submit myself to my brothers and sisters in the Lord. It will, in fact, become quite a problem for me if I don't submit. Let me give an example of a believer in submission to the church as a way of illustrating how church members should be submitted to each other:

Suppose, for example, I am the eldest son in the family and I am the only Christian in the family. Our father died a year ago and now on the first anniversary of his passing the family needs to do certain rituals on his behalf following their traditional animistic beliefs. As the eldest son of the family it is my responsibility to take the lead in the performance of these rituals. My uncles, the brothers of my father, have already reminded me of my responsibilities for the spirit-being of my father to carry out these rituals in order to avoid bringing the spirit's disastrous powers over the family if I fail to do them.

However, as a Christian, I know that I cannot participate in demonic rituals and attempt to communicate with the dead through sorcery. In the church we have been taught and we believe that the dead are in the hands of God, the righteous judge, and it is not our place as mortals to intervene on their behalf because their eternal destiny is not ours to determine.

As the time approaches for these rituals, my brothers in the church are aware of my dilemma, and several of them have counseled me about our faith in God in this matter and advised me concerning our understandings on this issue. They have expressed their solidarity with me as I face these difficult times. Because my faith in God is firm, because I am committed to shining the light of God's righteousness in all situations in my life and because the brothers and sisters of the church are with me in my commitment to following Jesus, I will be submissive to their direction rather than following the demonic traditions of my culture.

In being submissive to the church, I am likewise in submission to the power and Spirit of Christ (and vice-versa). In my submission and servanthood, I am opening the way for God's light to penetrate the darkness of my unbelieving family and further, into the broader community.

This is the great principle of godly subordination/submission/servanthood. One might call it resurrection subordination: the willingness to serve, suffer and even to die in fulfilling our role as a participant in God's eternal plan of salvation for his creation. In this life, as we submit to the body and to Christ the head of the body, we are assured of our ultimate and final exaltation with the triumphant, victorious Christ.

Willingness to be submitted to Christ and his body comes easily and naturally when three elements of our faith foundation are firmly in place:

1. Our eyes are focused on the future culmination of all things where there is the assured certainty of divine intervention and judgment.

2. Our submission to Christ opens the possibilities for transformation in the lives and situations of others.
3. The noblest disposition of a believer is to be daily following in the footsteps of our Master, Jesus Christ. When I share my own personal pilgrimage of coming to West Africa as a pioneer missionary, some people express amazement at my 'sacrifice' of leaving, family, friends and the comforts of an upcoming retirement in North America to come to spend the rest of my life where living conditions are at the lowest and most backward in the world. My response is only "um" because for me, to the contrary, it hasn't seemed like a sacrifice at all. It has been a golden, not-to-be-missed opportunity to actualize these three faith foundations. To have missed this auspicious journey would have been the profound tragedy of my life!

It is very important that we have a good comprehension of this fundamental discipleship principle as we move into the next chapter of "Household Codes" where submission and subordination are keywords.

## Reflection, discussion, action

1. Based on what you have read in this lesson, please list as many reasons as you can think of why it is of utmost importance to keep sexual relations strictly within the marriage covenant. I want reasons in addition to "because that is what the Bible says." Give me good solid theological, emotional and ethical reasons for faithfulness in marriage.

2. Why is our daily walk of faithfulness to Christ (sown in our conduct, attitudes and words) the best evangelism strategy available to us?

3. What are some of the things needing to be changed in your congregation to make it less compromised with darkness and become a stronger light to expose the darkness?

4. Explain to someone the essence of the principle of submission as taught in this lesson. Explain the submissiveness and servanthood of Christ and its importance in God's plan. Tell how submission to others can bring transformation to their lives.

# Lesson TEN

# The Household Codes
Ephesians 5: 22- 6:9

## Lesson 10 Passage overview

This section is known as "The Household Codes" and is found in several of the apostolic epistles. In the first century during the time when the epistles were written, the household was the extended family, the compound setting we are so familiar with here in Africa. And the extended family operated much like the typically patriarchal African family. In the New Testament era, the nuclear (husband, wife and children) family model was unheard of. Despite these similarities and differences, there is meaningful direction here for us today.

Verse 5:21 commands us to be filled with the Holy Spirit so that we are enabled to be subordinate to each other. We are subordinate and in submission to each other in the body of Christ enabling us to minister to each other and grow each other up into the fullness Christ, the true head. That is the responsibility a Christian husband has towards his wife and children, ministering to them and enabling them to grow up into maturity in Christ.

How does the husband lovingly minister to his wife?
- He loves her, giving himself to her, following the model of how Christ laid down his life for the benefit of the church.

- He helps her to reflect the holiness of God.
- He helps her understand the word and wisdom of God that cleanses her, enabling her to be holy and blameless.
- He loves, cherishes and cares for her just as he loves and cares for his own body.
- He is flawlessly faithful to her just as Christ is, was and always will be faithful to his bride, the church.
- He leaves his father's house to be join in a covenanted union with his wife.

In all the household/familial relationships, submission has a lot more to do with facilitating a person's movement up into Christ than it has to do with dominance and servile obedience.

(Please see page 18 in the section titled Words of Note.)

We closed the previous lesson with comments about the godly principle of submission, (that is coming under headship or authority of another) as the way of wisdom to realize God's design for walking in the light, coming into his fullness and sharing in Christ's exaltation.

The verses before us are identified as Household Codes. These codes were a normal part of instructional materials in the ancient world, both religious and secular. In that ancient context, the household continues to look and function very much like it does today in our West African setting. For us, a household is a collection of people living together in a compound where there is an organized social structure with lines of authority, work-sharing and mutual responsibilities among the residents. African households could scarcely function without their unwritten codes.

The household codes attached to several of the New Testament writings are practical guides for Christian conduct which can be easily understood and assimilated by African Christians. The first of the codes in Ephesians gives direction to the relationship between a Christian husband and wife.

## Husbands and wives- vv. 22-33

Verses 22 and 23 state unequivocally that a wife is to be submitted to her husband since he is her head. This could be read by some men as carte blanche power to have brute rule over the wife, to subjugate her and make her his fearful, personal slave. In many West African families, that is exactly the perception and reality of the relationship between a man and his wife.

That kind of a relationship between husband and wife is nothing more than a reflection of the husband's unredeemed carnality and is totally contrary to the biblical vision for a loving Christian marriage.

In scripture the word head is used in two senses: at times it designates status and authority over others; at other times it is used in the sense of source, goal and purpose. In this passage it is probably best to understand headship to be a blending of these two meanings.

There are good reasons for a somewhat softened understanding of headship in Christian marriage. One is that this section is introduced with the injunction that in the family of God we all are to be under submission to each other (5: 21). That injunction can be applied to all the relationships discussed in the remaining verses of the section, through 6:9.

Being submitted to each other means that we are ready and willing to serve one another, encourage each other and build one another up in the many ways that facilitate moving in the direction of Christ, our common head, our source of fullness and life itself.

It is a pleasure to see marriages that function like that; partners who have a profound appreciation for each other, they value each other and as they move through life together they support each other in realizing all the gifts and potential God has placed within them. In reality we often fall far short of that goal, but at least having that ideal out there is essential if we expect to move the marriage covenant in that direction.

Verse 25 quite explicitly draws the parallel of Christ in relation to the church and a husband in relation to his wife. Christ gave himself up (that is, sacrificed his very life) so that the church could be made into a bride of purity and beauty and worthy of Christ the bridegroom.

If we think that the wife is ordained to be submitted and obedient to her husband, the accompanying expectation for the husband to sacrifice himself for the wife so that she can be made holy and blameless is even more monumental.

How might a husband be in a servant relationship with his wife in ways that purify her and help to move her in the direction of Christ our head? The same question needs to be asked of his function as head of the family. How does the husband/father become a servant of the family, following the example of Christ who became a servant to all of us in the work of bringing all things under the authority of Messiah Jesus?

1. As he is deeply and intimately involved with her, he will understand her personality, her giftings, the call God has on her life and what are her deepest needs. That means spending much time with her, communicating with her and listening to her in loving, supportive sincerity.
2. He will be totally and faithfully committed to his wife as the one and only woman in his life in terms of emotional, romantic and sexual involvement.
3. He will share with her the heavy responsibilities of household duties, especially when children begin to join their union. This could include helping her with fetching water, finding firewood, cleaning the house, updating and maintenance of the house, gardening and food production, disciplining and caring for the children and probably many more tasks associated with family living.
4. He will free her to be with other women in Bible study and fellowship times.
5. He will encourage her to develop her own ministry gifts outside the home such as teaching children in the Christian education program of the church, visiting and ministering to the sick in the community and serving in church leadership.
6. When there is disagreement and conflict between husband and wife (as there inevitably will be), the wife will be given time to express her views so that together they will be able to find a way forward that is beneficial for unity and family well-being. Most women I have talked to have assured me

that when their husband is committed to them in these caring, supportive ways, being submissive to him is absolutely no problem! Ask your wife for her thoughts on this question.

The other half of this equation is the wife's responsibilities of being respectful and affirming of him in his responsibilities as leader and head for the family (v.33). The wife has a significant stake in making the relationship amicable and moving the family towards fullness in Christ:

1. She will be sensitive to her husband's need for intimacy, closeness and confidentiality with her.
2. She will have the family's care, well-being and nurture as a priority for her time and energies.
3. She will be committed to unity and harmony in the family.
4. She will be available to use her gifts in the ministry of the church and share God's love with women in the neighborhood.

Anthropologists, sociologists and other academicians would term this pattern of family life, subject to the father/male as head, as being patriarchal. For many moderns, Christian and unbelievers alike, the patriarchal model has been discarded as archaic and totally irrelevant. It has gone out to the trash heap along with dial telephones and floppy discs.

But, submission to headship is a proper ordering for both family and church life. It is a relational system that was in place since the beginning of time, untold millennia before modern enlightenment. For radical, biblical Christians it is a model of family life that is part of a much larger picture of God's blessing to mankind for a well-ordered society. Further, it mimics the manner in which God is reclaiming, recreating and saving his creation through his servant, Messiah Jesus. The true Messiah has become a suffering, sacrificial servant in obedience to the will of the Father as the path to the ultimate and universal Lordship as all things are gathered up into Christ. The husband becomes a servant to his family in his role of facilitating the family's movement towards the fullness of Christ. The wife, likewise, shares in this ministry through her submission and respect for her husband.

During the twentieth century it became apparent that some modifications in gender relationships were in order, specifically that male dominance had swung too far to the right, and women were suffering unjust and inhumane treatment in a society dominated by men. In the social upheavals of the 1960s, many Christians and churches joined the world in totally dumping this God-ordained principle. As a result of abandoning God's order for church and family life, the church in the West is now reaping a tragic harvest of disorder, division and social chaos. Let us be diligent in our teaching and pray that the church in Africa can avoid this error.

## Children, Parents and Fathers 6:1-4

As a child growing up in a Christian family, I had many occasions to be repeatedly reminded of verses 1-3. Now that I am much older and a father, myself, I know these verses are not just for young children. They are for anyone who has living parents. Children, regardless of their age, must always be respectful and solicitous to their parents. Times change, and it is not always reasonable for us to obey our parents in all the fine points when we are fifty as it was when we were five. Nevertheless, the respect and honor is there for the parents who brought us into the world and prepared us for adult life in the best way they knew at the time.

The fact that verse 1 is addressed to children suggests that the children are of such age that they are able to make this moral choice. Also the phrase "in the Lord" puts at least some limits on what parents can ask of children. If the parents are asking for obedience in an action that is not in the Lord then the children are not under obligation to obey. For example, we have seen parents forbidding their adult or young adult children to become disciples of Jesus. Obviously, that is an order that is not in the Lord.

Part of this code for children is especially directed at a father because of his primary responsibility for generating and promoting the moral and spiritual life of the family. He is commanded not to provoke the children to anger. If you recall from our study of the word "provoke" in 4:26, anger is allowed if it is directed at something that is inherently evil or unjust. Applying that understanding to this use of provoke in 6:4 means that a father should not do something unrighteous so as to cause his children alarm or to be troubled (provoked) at his misbehavior. If a father treats their mother with abuse and disrespect or if he is involved in a dishonest, fraudulent business transaction, for example, the children would have reason to be provoked at him. Thus, he should be a model of uprightness so as not to provoke the righteous indignation of his children. (This clause also suggests that the children are adults, or at least of the age of accountability.) It is particularly unsettling for adult children to observe their father (or mother for that matter) engaging in sub-Christian behavior.

This curb on the father also suggests that he should not demand the unquestioning and unqualified obedience of his children. Further, we understand that he, along with everyone else in the community of Christ, is accountable to each other through the covenant we have jointly made with Christ.

The final clause of this code brings additional clarity to the father's responsibility to his children: to "bring them up in the discipline and instruction of the Lord." The father (and no less, the mother) should be teaching and modeling for their children a life of obedience to Jesus and fear of our Almighty God. Zechariah, the father of John the Witness, quotes from the prophet Malachi in Luke 2:17-18, saying that his son will be instrumental "to turn the hearts of the fathers to the children, and the disobedient to the wisdom of the just, to make ready for the Lord a people prepared." Zechariah's vision for his son would be to prepare people for the Messianic kingdom of God through significant family relationships such as fathers with their children.

Psalm 127:3 tells us that children are a heritage from the Lord. I think it also appropriate to say that godly parents, as well, are part of a rich spiritual heritage. May God help us in this responsibility toward family.

## Slaves and Masters 6:5-9

These four verses giving direction to relations between slaves and their owner-masters reads as an anachronism to us. In our modern civil society, slavery (that is, keeping other persons as one's personal possession, against their wishes and forcing them to perform unremunerated labor) is repugnant, given our elevated regard for human value and rights. However in some darkest parts of the world slavery continues to be practiced with estimates of 20 to 30 million persons bound by real life slavery.

One wonders why the church of the first century didn't have the moral and social intuition to forthrightly abolish slavery. In reality, studying the code as stated here, slavery could not have continued because of the principle of subordination as detailed in these two lessons.

In the body of Christ we have shown we are to become servants (slaves) of each other. If a master becomes the slave of his slave and that slave, through transformation finds divine and eternal approval in his slavery, each gives his life for the other, the status of slave becomes moot. The social space, the dividing wall between master and slave, dissolves as both are moving upward and into the Head, Christ. Thus, while the instruction of the verses seems to miss us because none of us are either slave owners or a slave in involuntary bondage to a human master, there is, nevertheless, an important illustration here of how the subordination principle functions in God's mission of *gathering up all things into and under the Lordship of Christ.*

Please read the verses again from that perspective:

*Slaves, obey your earthly masters with fear and trembling, with a sincere heart, as you would Christ, not by the way of eye-service, as people-pleasers, but as servants of Christ, doing the will of God from the heart, rendering service with a good will as to the Lord and not to man, knowing that whatever good anyone does, this he will receive back from the Lord, whether he is a slave or free.*

The slave is transformed from the inhumane drudgery of constantly needing to please men and gaining nothing tangible or meaningful for all his efforts into becoming a servant of none other than the Lord and Master of time, eternity and all of Creation, thereby becoming a beneficiary of all the incomprehensible glories and riches of the Father.

For his part, the slave owner/master, in subordinating himself to his slave, is delivered from the slavery of his own flesh (a trafficker of his fellow humans) into being a slave of none other than the impartial, just and gracious Lord and Master of time, eternity and all of creation. As a result, the former master as well becomes a beneficiary of all the incomprehensible glories and riches of the Father.

Contemplate how both slave and master, through mutual subordination to each other and to Messiah Jesus, flow into God's eternal plan of doing his will on earth as it is in heaven and bringing all things under the Lordship of Christ. Allow your spirit to be overwhelmed by that plan and focus its meaning for your own life. As you do, you will begin to grasp the message, intent and import of the Epistle of Ephesians.

The code for masters and slaves carries important images and principles about Messiah Jesus and how his disciples are to imitate him. Consider first the status of a master. One becomes a master because of his fortuitous circumstances. He was born into wealth, he has a good education, he had technological advantages or he is in some way well connected. In other words, life has worked out for him that he is able to gain economic, social or political ascendency giving him power over others. If he manages his status to his advantage, he will have many people beholden to him and serving him.

The slave, by contrast, was born into poverty, he lacks education, and life for him is a non-stop struggle for survival. Out of dire necessity he sells himself and maybe even his family into unremunerated servitude to a master. Enter Messiah Jesus, a master beyond anything we can imagine. Leaving all his prestige and power behind, he comes as a slave with a special message to other slaves: "The Lord has sent me to proclaim liberty to the captives." He proceeds with that proclamation by setting many free with his power, and in the end he sacrifices his life in an act that forever cancels bondage to any who are willing to follow his example. Jesus put all his advantages as a master on the line in becoming a slave to mankind, thereby not just opening the gates to freedom from bondage; he utterly destroyed the gates!

Thus, the Jesus model is to sacrifice and submit oneself to the desire of the Father that his children are to be proclaimed free in Christ. We are faithful in carrying on his mission as we likewise lay down our lives, our talents, our advantages in proclaiming and inviting slaves into God's new order.

Many church leaders and pastors have it totally turned around from the Jesus model. For them, being a leader is the path to upward mobility, to becoming a master. But for disciples of Jesus, ministering for Jesus and the kingdom of God is the path into slavery, servanthood and sacrifice.

As we apprehend the godly destiny of this subordination principle, we can begin to apply it to our other relations highlighted in the Household Code: within the community of Christ, in the husband-wife relationship, in the parental relationship with children and even beyond these to any other relationship we have with others.

## Reflection, discussion and action

1. List several things you could do for your wife as her head or spiritual resource (or for a wife if you are not married). Let them be things that would purify her and help her to grow into Christ.

2. Is the African pattern of the domineering, demanding all-powerful father/husband the proper biblical model? If not, why not?

3. How does this lesson help you not to be a father who provokes his children? In what ways is fatherhood a kind of servant-hood?

4. Are you striving to be a master? What needs to change in your attitudes and actions that will enable you to become a Christlike servant?

# Lesson ELEVEN

# The Challenge to Divine Warfare
Ephesians 6: 10-20

## Lesson 11 Passage overview

After informing the church of God's salvation plan for eternity, recounting the blessings of being in Christ and how believers are on a journey of growing up into our head, the apostle concludes by summoning the church to join with God in the battle for the elevation of Christ to a place of supreme authority over all of creation.

Participation with God in his plan will require the body of Christ to go forth offensively, protected by the armor of the Divine Warrior himself. It is a picture of the church at the center of God's saving action. The church, like God, is offering men and women forgiveness, new life and hope, as well as doing battle with the cosmic powers which are resisting the gathering up of all things into Christ. In the Household Codes the apostle is telling the readers that even our normal social relationships of business and family are within the battlefield against the evil powers. Thus, it is required of us as a community to put on God's own protective armor. The church is protected with God's truth, justice, faith and eternal destiny as it announces the good news of peace.

Protestant preachers nearly always portray the individual Christian in the armor of God, doing battle. That is not the sense of Ephesians. Paul is telling us that we, as a community of faithful disciples, are together with God within his armor; the battle is a communal effort.

It is important to keep in mind that the letter to the Ephesians would have been read aloud to gathered congregations. This section, following the call to the church to be engaged with God in the battle against the forces of evil (Eph. 3:10-12), tells us how God does battle and equips the community of Christ to stand as witnesses against his enemies. Through their faithfulness in following in the footsteps of Jesus, growing up into the head, Christ, and now by putting on God's armor, the church is well prepared to join with him in the battle against the enemies of his salvation.

As background for this lesson it is most helpful for one to read Isaiah 59. This chapter is a prophecy concerning God's Messiah, the divine warrior (the new Moses) who comes to intervene on behalf of God's people, once again caught in bondage to God's enemies; a re-enactment of the Exodus narrative. In the Isaiah setting the components of the armor correspond to the ways the enemy has overcome God's people with untruth, injustice, unrighteousness, the absence of peace, covenant unfaithfulness and satanic bondage. The divine warrior does battle with the enemy on exactly these fronts as he intervenes to redeem God's people in Holy Spirit empowered covenant renewal.

The divine warrior's mission, in both Isaiah and Ephesians, portrays offensive spiritual warfare in the corporate or communal context. This encouraging prophecy is speaking to a gathered community rather than the typically defensive, individualistic, evangelical interpretation. The purpose of the passage is to inform us how the church is joined together with the divine warrior in offensive spiritual warfare with the objective of establishing God's kingdom in a hostile environment now under the control of Satan. Again, as often stated in this study guide, the Epistle of Ephesians demonstrates how the church is a partner in bringing all things, both in the heavenlies and on earth, under the dominion of Christ.

In verse 10, Paul, the great apostolic encourager, comes on strong with, "Finally [or, better translated as henceforth] be **strong** in the Lord and in the strength of his **might**." This power admonition echoes that of I Cor. 16:13: "Be **watchful**, stand *firm* in the faith, act like **men**, and be **strong**".

Verse 11 instructs us to put on the very armor of God. Some expositors use the example of the individual Christian metaphorically donning the war gear of a Roman soldier. It is better to understand Paul's point that believers need to inhabit the armor the divine warrior himself wears. Taking counsel and doing battle from within the divine armor, we are assured of being "able to stand against the schemes of the devil." The picture is of Christians within God's armor, embattled but enabled to outwit, stay ahead of and be aware of the deceptive, crafty methods Satan uses in attempting to thwart or undo God's saving mission for his creation. It is clearly a spiritual battle, not literal warfare against a human enemy. In relation to human enemies, whom Satan uses in his schemes, Christians love them, offering healing and life. God never expects us to carry on warfare against other humans. When Satan uses people in his tactics, as is often the case, the temptation is to see them as our enemy rather than victims of Satan.

The list of spiritual powers with whom we do battle in v. 12 is awesome: rulers, authorities, cosmic powers and spiritual forces of evil in the heavenly places. The fact that they also are in the heavenlies is indicative of their lofty stature. They are in high places of authority over the affairs of mankind, human institutions and the power organization throughout the cosmos. Christ the victor, now and eternally, is subjecting all powers and authorities to himself, therefore, there can be nothing left outside this list of opponents to the saving design of God. That helps us to understand the magnitude of our calling to be joined together with Christ in his ascendency to exaltation. We are not called simply to stand our ground and observe the battle; we are enlisted to join with him in resisting the opponent.

Being able to withstand in the evil day likely means the church's ability to do battle every day until all things are gathered up under the authority of Christ. The first two words of v. 14, "stand therefore" could have reference to ancient warfare strategy: the combatants still upright and standing on their feet at the end of the day are the recognized victors. At the end of the battle, that's where we want to be: still standing!

## Components of the armor
## The belt of truth

Truth, as used here, goes beyond simply the absence of lying speech. Truth is embodied and on display in the community of Christ, the earthly representative of God's truth in all its fullness. The truth of God stands in opposition to the powers of evil; they owe their existence to lies. Evil power is built on a foundation of lies, untruths and twisted truth. Lies are the primary nourishment of evil.

Here are some of the more prominent lies holding sway over West Africa:

1. God exists, but he is far away and removed from our world. He is of little consequence in our daily affairs, but maybe he can occasionally help make something good happen, as in the oft repeated phrase, "If the good Lord wills it." The lie is that real spiritual power in our world is the domain evil spirits, witchcraft and marabous, not God.
2. Women and children are of less value than men.
3. Fate, fortune and power over others are had through the manipulation of evil spirits.
4. Healing is sooner found through witchcraft than through modern medical care.
5. Fraud and thievery are ok as long as you don't get caught.
6. Black people are inferior, less competent and less intelligent than white people.
7. Burning vegetative materials from the past growing season adds fertility to the soil.
8. Violence is the most effective way of controlling others.

There is even a list of lies that have been accepted into the life and teachings of some churches:

It is acceptable for church leaders to use verbal and even physical abuse against believers who are judged to be disobedient to church authorities, especially unsubmissive wives.

It is more important to preach the wrath, vengeance and punishment of God than to portray him as a longsuffering, forgiving, patient, gracious and kind loving Father.

A track to upward mobility, wealth and power is yours by becoming a big-man pastor. The congregation's responsibility is to serve the pastor rather than the reverse.

A fast track to hell is for those who fail to pay their tithe.

Sickness and poverty are signs of not being in right relationship with God.

The best way to demonstrate your faith and spirituality is by putting on a dramatic show during the Sunday morning service.

The most important reason for becoming a Christian is so that I gain access to heaven when I die. To make that happen, all I need to do is believe Jesus died on the cross to cancel the guilt of my on-going sinful way of living.

Satan is having a heyday in West Africa because of the prominence of these lies and probably many more that could be listed. But in the faithful community of Christ, the way believers conduct their lives shines the light of God's truth into everyone of these lies showing them to be false.

When Christians wear the belt of truth, which enables them to live by God's truth and imitate and reflect the glory of Christ, the powers of darkness will retreat and run for cover.

God is *true and right*. We receive and walk in his truth in so far as we are obedient to God's revelation to us through his Son, Messiah Jesus. When we, as a community of Christ, are wrapped in God's truth like a belt around our middle, our clothing and armor stay up where they belong, giving us protection in the battle against the enemy. But when we let slide this revealed protective truth from God, we become open and vulnerable to attacks by the enemy. Please understand the belt of truth to be all that we have received through Jesus about God and how that truth about God enables us to live and walk the way he desires for his chosen people. If you look at the lists of lies, you will see how, when those untruths creep into our lives and our churches, we begin to lose power and the enemy gains ground in the battle. Not having a belt of righteousness might be illustrated in the attire of some young men nowadays. Either they have no belt on their trousers or the belt that's there is not intended to be effective. Their trousers are always sliding down, and as they go along they are constantly obliged to keep pulling them back up. They find it difficult to work or be engaged with the task at hand because they are forever occupied with concern that their trousers are sliding down too far.

## The breastplate of righteousness

The Greek biblical word *dikaiosune* is translated into English either as justice or righteousness. For a better understanding of what the apostle has in mind, we need to go back to his source of the armor image in Isaiah 59. There the prophet describes unrighteousness/injustice as people whose works are *works of iniquity and deeds of violence are in their hands. Their feet run to evil, and they are swift to shed innocent blood; their thoughts are thoughts of iniquity* (vv. 6-7), *Justice is turned back, and righteousness stands far away; for truth has stumbled in the public squares, and uprightness cannot enter* (v.17). God's warrior, viewing rampant injustice among the people, sees that no one is intervening on behalf of those suffering from the unrighteous behavior. At that point he puts on the breastplate of righteousness and goes into action on behalf of those suffering injustice.

In our world one of the key methods Satan uses in appealing to people is pulling them into the abuse of power, into a life that condones injustice for the sake of personal gain. That is a key place where God desires to have the witness and action of his church take up the breastplate of righteousness and justice on behalf of persons under attack from the enemy in this way.

Unrighteous and unjust actions are everywhere a part of West African life. I know of a powerful government leader who caused the death of a woman through an act of violence with his own hands. Because this man had a family member high up in the justice system, his crime was simply wiped out and he suffered no consequences. I know of another man whose feet were running to evil and he bought off a judge in an attempt to clear his thievery. In other cases, it is the person who gets money into the hand of the police officer first who gets the judgment in his favor, regardless of who really is innocent or guilty.

God's primary witness against the unrighteous and unjust behavior in our culture is his church. We are under the protection of his shield of righteousness and justice, and we need to be intervening on behalf of those whose rights and dignity are stumbling in the public squares. Every congregation should have those who are watching for people whose rights are being ignored and who are ready to offer comfort and support to those suffering from injustice.

## Feet equipped with the gospel of peace

The Segond 21 (French) Bible version provides an energizing rendition of this verse as, *"put on your feet, shoes of zeal in the proclamation of the gospel of peace."*

The linking of feet and the gospel as a message of peace is drawn from the Messianic prophecy of Isaiah 52:7 (also my favorite verse of the Old Testament): *"How beautiful upon the mountains are the feet of him who brings good news, who publishes peace, who brings good news of happiness, who publishes salvation, who says to Zion, 'Your God reigns!'"*

The author of Ephesians has already identified Messiah Jesus as the great messenger of peace, as we have noted in chapter 2: *"For he himself is our peace, who has made us both one and has broken down in his flesh the dividing wall of hostility"* (v.14) and *... that he might create in himself one new man in place of the two, so making peace, and might reconcile us both to God in one body through the cross, thereby killing the hostility.*

*And he **came** and preached peace to you who were far off and peace to those who were near* (vv. 15-17). The sense of this passage is that the gospel of peace is mobile and offensive; it is being carried by specially protected human feet into enemy territory.

Still, there is something of a war versus peace paradox in this verse: The message of peace equips and protects the divine warrior (and us, his troops) as we confront the enemies of God. While the enemy wages warfare and destruction against God's saving activity, we confront the enemy with the bold message of the Messiah who wages peace, who has brought us together in peace and who declares peace between former enemies.

In West Africa the gospel of peace is like *A word fitly spoken... like apples of gold in a setting of silver (Proverbs 25:11)*. Many in West Africa have lived with on-going conflicts, suffering through years of bloodshed and rebellions. Others are deep into family and clan conflicts where evil powers and curses are piled up against the opposing sides. In most communities violence against women and children is accepted as normal.

I am always impressed by the testimonies of people who become disciples of Jesus in this culture of violence; they freely and honestly share how they have been set free from cyclical conflict and the obligation to repay evil with evil. In Christ they have found liberty; the overcoming power of sharing Divine peace with their enemies.

## The shield of faithfulness

The shield of faith(fullness) is both defensive and offensive, enabling the warrior to *extinguish all the flaming darts of the evil one*. This evokes scenes from ancient battle strategy whereby the enemy would propel burning projectiles into their opponent's city in an effort to ignite destructive fires. The shield intercepted and extinguished these flaming projectiles causing them to fall harmlessly to the ground without doing their intended damage.

As the church is faithful, obedient and following after Jesus, we have this protection of his armor. Anyone who has engaged in the mission to establish communities of faith in an animistic or any other anti-Christian setting knows exactly what it is like to be under attack of fiery darts from the spiritual opposition.

We have seen, for example, how the enemy can bring unbelievers into the community of faith—people who give the pretense of being believers but in reality are wolves, dressed up like sheep. They give the appearance of belonging to the flock when in reality they have a totally different agenda for being there.

We have also seen how Satan marshals his agents to bring false accusations against believers, spreading rumors in the community for the purpose of creating mistrust of Christians. Other times the enemy, through his human agents, has attempted to engender fear in the community of faith through loud intimidation and threats against us. Still another fiery dart is the satanic effort to bringing disunity into the body of Christ. Division in the body can be very destructive. In all these attacks we come through as victors provided we remain faithful and obedient in following the way of suffering after our Lord. It is awesome to stand by and watch the various ways the warrior shield extinguishes these fiery attacks:

The enemy is thrown into confusion, even turning against itself.

The good works of the faithful bring overwhelming testimony against the attacks. Wolves have simply slinked away into the bush, in shame at their defeat.

The community of faith quickly learns the importance of solidarity amongst themselves.

Fair-minded unbelievers will even come to the defense of the faith community.

What a mighty God we serve!

## The helmet of salvation

The helmet, similar to the shield is something one takes up, as stated here. Salvation refers not only to our own personal salvation (as in the personal, individualist interpretation) but also salvation as the foremost characteristic of our message. Through Messiah Jesus and the church, God is offering salvation to his creation and the entire cosmos. Salvation is both mission and message. It is the grand project of God that fully engages us, his people. Salvation stands in bold contrast to the opposing option: loss, destruction, corruption and death. Salvation is liberation from the fate of those opposed to God and his Christ.

One of the most perplexing, unfathomable struggles faced by believers is how their family and friends can opt to stay on the road to destruction even when they have seen and understand the change that has transpired in the lives of believers so close to them.

## The sword of the Spirit, the word of God

In 1 Cor. 12, the Spirit is the empowering, revealing presence of God among the believers to carry on the work and ministry of

Christ. The Spirit empowers us with wisdom, knowledge, faith, healing, miracles, prophecy and more.

For many generations of Christians, the phrase "word of God" has meant the written scripture, the biblical text. But for Paul and the early Christians to whom Ephesians was written, the "word" referred to the full range of ways that God speaks or otherwise reveals himself to the world and his people, but principally through the life, teachings and exaltation of Messiah Jesus. It is this word that accompanies us into the battle against the enemies of God's salvation. Other texts help us to understand the significance and power of this weapon:

Hebrews 4:12-13 "For the word of God is living and active, sharper than any two-edged sword, piercing to the division of soul and of spirit, of joints and of marrow, and discerning the thoughts and intentions of the heart. And no creature is hidden from his sight, but all are naked and exposed to the eyes of him to whom we must give account.

Revelation 19:13-17[The rider on the white horse] "is clothed in a robe dipped in blood, and the name by which he is called is **The Word of God**. And the armies of heaven, arrayed in fine linen, white and pure, were following him on white horses. From his mouth comes a *sharp sword* with which to strike down the nations, and he will rule them with a rod of iron. He will tread the winepress of the fury of the wrath of God the Almighty. On his robe and on his thigh he has a name written, King of kings and Lord of lords." Surrounded with a weapon and armor like that, who or what is to be feared? Nothing!

## Pray and persevere

If we are inclined to read the Bible as a collection of random spiritual tidbits, then verses 17-20 are another of those pithy sound bites; this one encourages believers to pray. On the other hand, if we read the Bible in its context and wholeness, and as intelligently related thoughts, then these verses round out the apostle's outline of the divine warrior's and the Christian community's battle preparation. We take these verses in the latter sense.

Prayer is the joining of our personal and corporate spirit with the Holy Spirit in the sense of awareness, sensitivity and openness to the will, the desire and the plan of God for this time and place. It is through prayer that we engage with the dvine warrior in the battle against wickedness in both the high and the low places. It is an engagement also in time, that one is vigilant and watching for opportunities to bring God's light of truth and justice into the darkness.

Prayer may include verbalization on our part, but keeping alert with perseverance (v.18) suggests that prayer is an on-going relationship with the Holy Spirit: listening, watching and sensitivity to what, where and how the divine warrior is leading. It's much more that we are placing ourselves in a position of availability and following after God than for us to be telling him what to do next. He is bringing all things under the authority of Christ, and is directing his faithful community, the church, to engage offensively and defensively in the advancement of his kingdom. Prayer is the communicating link keeping us in touch with the divine battle strategy. God has already told us what needs to be done in terms of bringing his light into the darkness. The much more significant question is "are we available to do what He has already told us needs to happen?" In verses 19-20, Paul asks his listeners to be in that attitude of prayer on his behalf, that God would give him the words to speak in the proclamation of the mystery of the gospel which he summarizes so eloquently in 3:9-10. Note that the objective is the words God has given him, not the words he gives God. Paul is well aware of God's battle plan; he asks only for the sensitivity and boldness to be God's ambassador in chains.

At the end of the epistle, Paul caps it off with this statement of self-perception as a church leader that, here in West Africa, we do well to heed. On the lofty side, he is none other than an ambassador, representing the everlasting King of kings and Lord of lords. But in his latest reality check the sublime ambassador is chained to the walls of a filthy, vermin ridden cell in a Roman prison. Running vividly through his mind are the ups and downs of the past twenty years of missionary work: "as servants of God we commend ourselves in every way: by great endurance, in afflictions, hardships, calamities, beatings, imprisonments, riots, labors, sleepless nights, hunger; by purity, knowledge, patience, kindness, the Holy Spirit, genuine love; by truthful speech, and the power of God; with the weapons of righteousness for the right hand and for the left; through honor and dishonor, through slander and praise. We are treated as impostors, and yet are true; as unknown, and yet well known; as dying, and behold, we live; as punished, and yet not killed; as sorrowful, yet always rejoicing; as poor, yet making many rich; as having nothing, yet possessing everything" (2 Cor.6:4-10).

For Jesus, Paul, and the innumerable host of God's servants who have followed their example, the path to exaltation must invariably pass through a lifetime of suffering, servitude and eventually the giving of life itself. This is the master model to whom Paul was discipled, with these suggestions on how we might imitate him: "in humility count others more significant than yourselves. Let each of you look not only to his own interests, but also to the interests of others. Have this mind among yourselves, which is yours in Christ Jesus, who, though he was in the form of God, did not count equality with God a thing to be grasped, but made himself nothing, taking the form of a servant, being born in the likeness of men. And being found in human form, he humbled himself by becoming obedient to the point of death, even death on a cross" (Phil. 2:3-8).

## Reflection, discussion, action

1. Which interpretation of the warrior's armor do you prefer—the individualistic or the communitarian? Explain the difference between the two understandings. Explain why you prefer one interpretation more than the other.

2. What are some common lies that people live by in your neighborhood?

3. Explain the difference between warfare with flesh and blood and warfare against spiritual forces, principalities and powers.

4. List some of the evil powers in the community where you live. In what ways is your faith community engaged in battle to defeat them? As you pray, how is God directing and empowering your faith community to struggle against these powers?

## Closing remarks and benediction

Paul closes this epistle in the style typical for ancient letters. There is the mutual concern for each other's well-being and a desire to maintain the communal ties over the long separation. This takes us back to a time long before postal service and other ways we moderns stay in touch. Messages were hand-carried by trusted servants and co-workers. But the human sentiments and feelings of community are still there.

The last two sentences are loaded with four words that are common from Paul's pen and that come naturally from one with apostolic responsibilities for churches: love, faith, grace, and peace. All are keywords in the Christian's vocabulary and all are essential attributes of God's covenant people who are engaged in his great plan for time and eternity: bringing all things together under the Lordship of Christ.

## Appendix A

# Constantinianism's Impact on Church History; the Anabaptist Alternative

A fundamental change in the Christian church happened during the fourth and fifth centuries AD. In church history this shift is known as Constantinianism, named after Constantine, the Roman emperor at the time when the Christian church was granted official toleration by the Roman government. In fact, Christianity soon became the established religion of the Roman Empire. The change process actually began before his reign (306-337 AD) and its influence continues even to this day in the phenomenon known as Christendom.

Constantinianism reflects the change in the status of the church from a scarcely tolerated and often persecuted missionary minority movement based on the apostles and prophets of the first century gathered around Jesus Christ as it transitioned into an established socio/political institution. Once linked to the Roman Empire, the church became a wealthy, powerful entity with the authority to regulate life within its own ranks as well as in general society backed by the power of the state.

In the process of this change the ethics and doctrines of the church were gradually adjusted from that of Christ and the apostles to reflect the requirements of the new reality. The emperor himself became a Christian and exerted his power on behalf of the church; all society was christened.

Having received the support of the political authorities and interpreting this support as providential, the church was forced to adjust its hermeneutics to reflect the new status quo. Hermeneutics are the methods, principles and guidelines for interpreting the Bible into the life of the community of Christ.

It then became expedient for the church leadership to interpret the Bible in such a way as to maintain the new order which benefited both church and state. The resulting hermeneutical changes became established as orthodox, providing ways of evading challenges and offering reinforcement of the new system.

This situation was totally different from the vision of Christ in Mark 10:42-45: "Jesus called the disciples to him and said to them, "You know that those who are considered rulers of the Gentiles lord it over them, and their great ones exercise authority over them. But it shall not be so among you. But whoever would be great among you must be your servant, and whoever would be first among you must be slave of all. For even the Son of Man came not to be served but to serve, and to give his life as a ransom for many."

The changes were especially dramatic in the social ethics of Christians. For example, at the beginning of the fourth century, believers refused to participate in military service for the government. But by the beginning of the fifth century, those who participated in the Roman army were **required** to be Christians.

During this period the meaning of being a Christian was gradually changed. Rather than being a movement of Christlike people, the church was anyone who confessed the Apostles Creed, who forensically acknowledged the scriptures and who obeyed the apostolic successor, the bishop of Rome.

Because so few Christians were actually converted, it was soon recognized that it would be impractical to require the whole population to accept New Testament ethics, so Old Testament norms were adopted for all except the monastic orders and the clergy. Church leaders also realized that the New Testament provided no guidelines for organizing the kind of sacral society or hierarchical church which was emerging. But since Christendom more closely resembled the theocracy of the Old Testament, the authority of the Old Testament grew and much New Testament teaching tended to be regarded as applicable only in the religious orders, in the eschatological future kingdom, or as unreachable ideals.

In particular, the increasing distance between Jesus' lifestyle and that of church leaders necessitated the diminishing importance of the humanity of Jesus. It was no longer acceptable to see him as the human example Christians should imitate. Consequently, in the fourth century, Jesus was recast as a celestial figure, his divinity was emphasized and the memory of a radical Messiah Jesus was allowed to fade.

Significant change also happened in the understanding of salvation and the saving work of Christ. The benefits of the saving work of Christ became vested in the communion elements and received by simply going through the ritualized communion service. Baptism and communion became the sacraments whereby one became a Christian and received God's grace; the spiritual and moral transformation of the saving work of Christ was no longer thought necessary for the laity of the church.

Instead, the saving, transforming work of Christ was interpreted as an abstract saving forensic transaction up in heaven. This allowed for sinful and violent people and corrupt structures to remain essentially unchanged. The literal, ethical components of Christ's teaching and saving work withered away, and the transcendent aspects, especially of his sacrifice and expiation, were raised up because they more easily lent themselves to sacramental expression. Un-Christlike people could thereby be assured of the benefits of the saving death of Christ, without bothering with the discipled, transformation of one's conduct.

The reign of Christ was declared to have already arrived on earth in the form of the establishment of the Christian religion. Constantine, the most gracious Christian king, could be regarded as the Vicar of Christ on earth. The cosmic theology, which regarded Jesus as the incarnation of the Cosmic Logos, could be used to integrate the political realm with the cosmic. The Christian emperor, with the Christian bishop at his right hand, became the new Vicar of Christ on earth, governing the Christian state of the new redeemed order of history!

When one analyzes fourth century creeds, hymns, church calendars and catechisms, much change is evident. These primary sources demonstrate an abandonment of the previously held Christocentric biblical interpretation. In the new order of the church, the life of Christ was used devotionally rather than ethically. These same sermons and other writings demonstrate the disappearance of the distinction between church and world.

Major New Testament themes such as the kingdom of God no longer seemed significant. The Great Commission seemed to have been fulfilled.

The presuppositions of Christendom were not significantly challenged until the advent of the Enlightenment and Protestant Reformation of the sixteenth century. Between the fourth until the sixteenth century, there were some challenges to the corruption brought by the unholy alliance of church and state under the Holy Roman Empire, but these voices of dissent were vigorously and violently dealt with as heresy by the ecclesiastical/political Powers.

This was the situation, both politically and hermeneutically, that faced Reformers and Anabaptists in the sixteenth century. The Protestant Reformers initially criticized blatant abuses and immorality in the Church without urging schism. However, they eventually accepted the inevitability of separation and, having secured the support of certain political authorities, set up alternative expressions of Christendom that removed objectionable features but maintained the basic Christendom in a Protestant context.

The Protestant Reformers such as Luther, Zwingli and Calvin, introduced changes, but they did not abandon the Christendom mindset which had dominated biblical interpretation for centuries. By rejecting the monastic options, they did remove the two-tier approach to discipleship, but they did not reassert New Testament morality as the standard. By emphasizing justification by faith, they focused attention on the New Testament and on Jesus as redeemer, but they would not allow Jesus to be normative for ethics and the Christian's lifestyle. Though they insisted on the freedom of biblical interpretation free from the scrutiny of political or ecclesiastical authorities, in practice they continued to rely on the enforcement powers of state authorities. Their attempts to apply scripture to the whole of life were undermined by their wariness of interpretations that might threaten the social, political and economic status quo. And they continued to find the Old Testament guidelines beneficial for the new Protestant Christendom they built.

Anabaptists realized that simply reforming the state church system was inadequate and that forming believers' churches was essential. They comprehensively rejected Christendom and its symbols. This radical stance enabled them to interpret scripture in new ways. They too rejected two-tier Christianity with different standards and callings for different Christians, but, unlike the Reformers, they chose to apply New Testament standards to all Christians. Instead of two-tier Christendom, they recovered the "two kingdoms" approach of the New Testament and argued that, for Christians, Jesus was the norm for ethics as well as salvation. The Old Testament might still be relevant within society, but within believers' churches the New Testament governed ecclesiology and ethics. New Testament teachings were to be obeyed whatever their social implications. Anabaptists rejected, for example, interpretations of Romans 13 that required excessive deference to the political authorities and they operated not with a "hermeneutics of order" but with a "hermeneutics of obedience".

Unlike the Reformers, they were not in a dominant position. Their position seemed analogous to the persecuted churches of the first three centuries, and their interpretation of scripture resembled the primitive church, pre-Christendom interpretations more than those of the Reformers or most interpreters since Constantine.

The implications for hermeneutics of the Anabaptists' rejection of Christendom were profound and led to the development of an approach to biblical interpretation that was very different from that of the Reformers, an approach that resulted in alternative perspectives, especially on ethical issues and ecclesiology.

## Appendix B

# An Overview of Anabaptist Hermeneutics

Those who have examined the hermeneutics of the Anabaptists have identified six key components:

1. **The Bible as Self-interpreting**
2. **Christocentrism**
3. **The Two Testaments**
4. **Spirit and Word**
5. **Congregational Hermeneutics**
6. **Hermeneutics of Obedience**

In exploring the contemporary significance of Anabaptist hermeneutics, we welcome Anabaptists as conversation-partners, learning both from the hermeneutical principles which seem to have been widely adopted by them and from the creative tension evident in the conversations which took place as they debated hermeneutical questions. These six principles do not stand alone but overlap and mutually reinforce or qualify each other.

## 1. Scripture as Self-interpreting

The widespread Anabaptist conviction was that scripture was clear enough for ordinary Christians to understand and apply without assistance of educational, philosophical or theological expertise, clerical guidance or ecclesiastical tradition. They believed that difficult passages would be illuminated by clearer ones.

Scripture was clear, they taught, when it was read under the intuition of the Holy Spirit. Such clarity could not be expected, however, by those who neglected the Spirit's help. Many Anabaptists insisted that they relied on the Holy Spirit as the interpreter who would lead believers into the truth and whose teaching was more helpful than education or theological expertise.

Most Anabaptists regarded scripture as Christocentric, treating the words and example of Jesus as the clearest and most accessible portion of scripture. All other passages were interpreted in the light of this. They acknowledged that the Old Testament was less easy to interpret, requiring careful handling lest it detract from the centrality of Jesus and the radical newness of the new covenant. But since Christians were no longer under the old covenant, many argued, they could concentrate on the New Testament and use it to explain the Old Testament. In practice, therefore, not all of scripture was clear, but guided by the principle of Christocentrism, ordinary believers could use the Bible with confidence.

## 2. Christocentrism

The centrality of Jesus in scripture was foundational for Anabaptist hermeneutics and theology. Jesus Christ is regarded as the one to whom all scripture pointed and witnessed, and his words and deeds are authoritative and normative. The conviction that this part of scripture was the clearest of all (though also the most demanding) meant that the principles of Christocentrism and the clarity of Scripture overlapped and reinforced each other. So fundamental was this principle of Christocentrism in Anabaptist hermeneutics that it tended to qualify other hermeneutical elements.

From this Anabaptist conviction that Jesus Christ was pivotal to biblical revelation flowed the priority they accorded to the New Testament. Most were convinced that the new covenant he introduced made it impossible to put the Old Testament on the same level as the New. Although many acknowledged the essential unity of Scripture, the Anabaptists' Bible was not flat, and many emphasized the discontinuity between the Testaments.

Two other convictions, however, qualified this focus on the New Testament and helped to prevent them discarding the Old. First, the emphasis on the clarity and self-interpreting nature of scripture prevented them from emphasizing the discontinuity of the testaments. If Scripture is self-interpreting, it must have a basic unity and coherence. Provided the two Testaments were not confused, much spiritual benefit, albeit of a devotional nature, could be gained from the Old Testament. Also, reliance on the Spirit encouraged some Anabaptists to reclaim the Old Testament using allegorical methods.

## 4. Spirit and Word

The use of allegorization was one element in the debate about Spirit and Word that characterized the early Reformation period. Anabaptists were committed both to the normative role of Scripture and to the active involvement of the Holy Spirit in the process of interpretation.

Their emphasis on the role of the Spirit was tempered by some of their other convictions. First, their belief that scripture was essentially plain and self-interpreting discouraged them from adopting speculative interpretations under the supposed influence of the Spirit's illumination. Common sense and the obvious meaning of the text were not easily rejected in favor of more esoteric or supposedly spiritual meanings. Second, their Christocentrism meant that any supposed guidance from the Spirit had to be squared with the teaching and example of Jesus. They acknowledged that the Holy Spirit was the Spirit of Jesus and that he would not teach them anything inconsistent with what Jesus had taught.

## 5. Congregational Hermeneutics

They believed that the congregation was where scripture should be interpreted, rather than the university, the preacher's study or the mind of the individual. However, this too must be understood in the context of other important convictions.

These primarily concern the nature of the hermeneutic community, which was understood as both a charismatic community and a community of disciples. The Anabaptist emphasis on the role of the Spirit meant that only in a congregation where there was freedom for the Sprit to guide individuals and unite the community around the Word would they be able to operate properly as a hermeneutic community. And the Anabaptist emphasis on obedience as a prerequisite for understanding Scripture meant that only a community of would-be disciples could expect illumination. Unfaithfulness could make a congregation unable to function properly as a hermeneutic community.

## 6. Hermeneutic of Obedience

The importance attached to ethical considerations in interpreting scripture, both in the legitimizing of interpreters and the testing of their conclusions, is clear from Anabaptist writings. However, this principle overlapped with others in certain ways which in some measure qualified it.

First, the ethical presuppositions by which they tested both interpreters and their interpretations were, at least in theory, not free-standing but derived from their Christocentrism. This was necessary if their commitment to *sola scriptura* was not to be compromised by importing an ethical norm that somehow stood over against scripture. Thus, the ethical focus needed to be subordinate to their Christocentrism.

Briefly stated, the model that can be derived from Anabaptist hermeneutical principles and practices is that of Spirit-filled disciples, confidently interpreting scripture within a community of likeminded disciples, aware that Jesus Christ is the centre from which the rest of scripture must be interpreted.

We live in a post-Christendom culture, a post-modern culture and a post-colonial culture (among many other "post" words we could use). We need a hermeneutic that is appropriate to meet the challenges and opportunities of this culture. The radical tradition offers a Jesus-centered hermeneutic in a post-Christendom culture, especially where the institutional church is declining but where the teaching and example of Jesus might be alternatively attractive. It offers a communal hermeneutic in an individualistic post-modern culture where fragmentation has become an art form but where community is desperately needed as the context within which meaning can be discovered.

In West Africa we sense a cry of renewal and revival of the church. We propose consideration of the radical Anabaptist model as a tool that will help us arrive at the rediscovery and redefining of the Christian community we so eagerly desire. May God help us.

*Material for Appedices A and B was compiled from the writings of Anabaptist scholars, Stuart Williams and John Driver. For more information visit www.anabaptistnetwork.org*

# Appendix C

# Figures

## Figure 1 **Faith Intinerary**

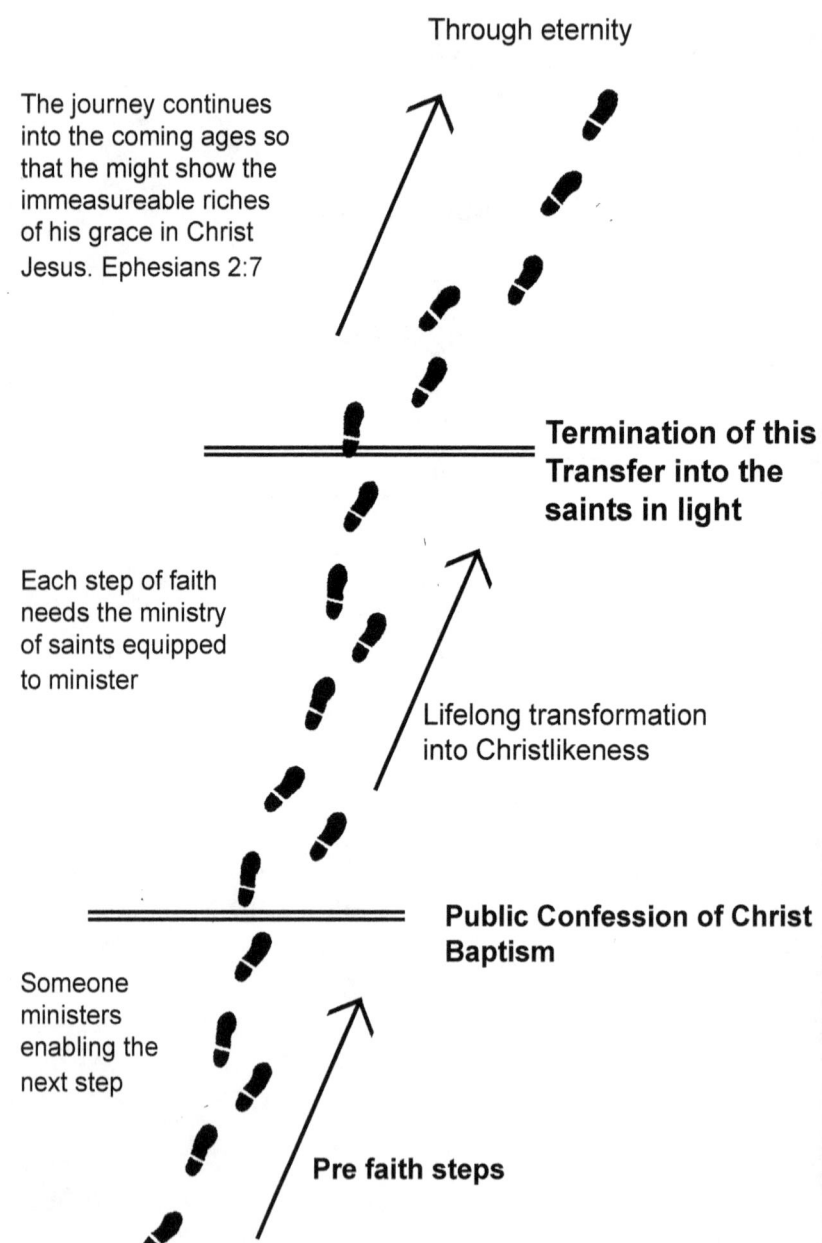

## Figure 1 **Faith Itinerary**

This chart shows an individual's faith development as he transitions from unbelief to conversion, followed by transformation into Christlikeness throughout one's lifetime and finally arriving in glory when this life is ended. But even at that juncture, spiritual development continues on into the celestial realm throughout eternity.

At the bottom of the chart, prior to conversion, there are small steps of faith that bring one into contact with the message of God's salvation. These first steps towards faith could be the witness of a Christian friend, a God encounter such as a dream or vision or a miraculous intervention that draws one's attention and interest towards the Lord. This stage can last several days or even several years.

At some point, however, provided he continues to move forward towards Jesus, one's faith reaches a point where he is able to respond positively to God's invitation to become a disciple of Jesus. With this response the individual is converted, he abandons the way of sin and Satan and he publically proclaims, through the rite of baptism with water that he is now a child of God, and his heart is set on of being a disciple of Jesus. Conversion occurs when one becomes born anew through the power of the Holy Spirit and begins to understand how God is transforming his life into one directed from above, instead of by the flesh. Through each step of faith maturation, he becomes more and more like Jesus.

In the radical church tradition, the faith itinerary occurs in the context of Christian community rather than in an isolated, private relationship with God. In Christian community we serve each other, being mutually submitted to each other as we walk together into fullness and maturity in Christ. As one is ministered to by the gifts within the body, he matures in his Christlikeness and is thereby empowered to minister to others, both within and outside the community.

The manner in which biblical teaching is screened through preaching, worship, traditions, rituals and doctrine can promote, inhibit or even block spiritual development along the faith itinerary towards the purposes of God. If one is in a church context where biblical truth is ignored, excluded, distorted or disobeyed, one's spiritual development can be seriously impeded.

The leaders in the body of Christ are essentially equippers, enabling others to minister, for example, as pastors, teachers, apostles and prophets. Leaders in the body are not masters, lording it over the body; they are simply servants laying down their lives so that others will find new life in Christ.

The Bible gives us scant details on what happens when this mortal life is finished and we graduate into the next phase of our oneness in Christ. But the Apostle Paul gives us a hint at what is in store for the faithful disciple of Jesus in a free quote from the prophet Isaiah: "What no eye has seen, nor ear heard, nor the heart of man imagined, what God has prepared for those who love him," these things God has revealed to us through the Spirit. (1 Cor. 2:9-10, cf. 1 Cor. 15). Paul asserts that it is going to take ages for God to show us the immeasurable riches of his grace and kindness toward us in Christ Jesus (Eph. 2:7).

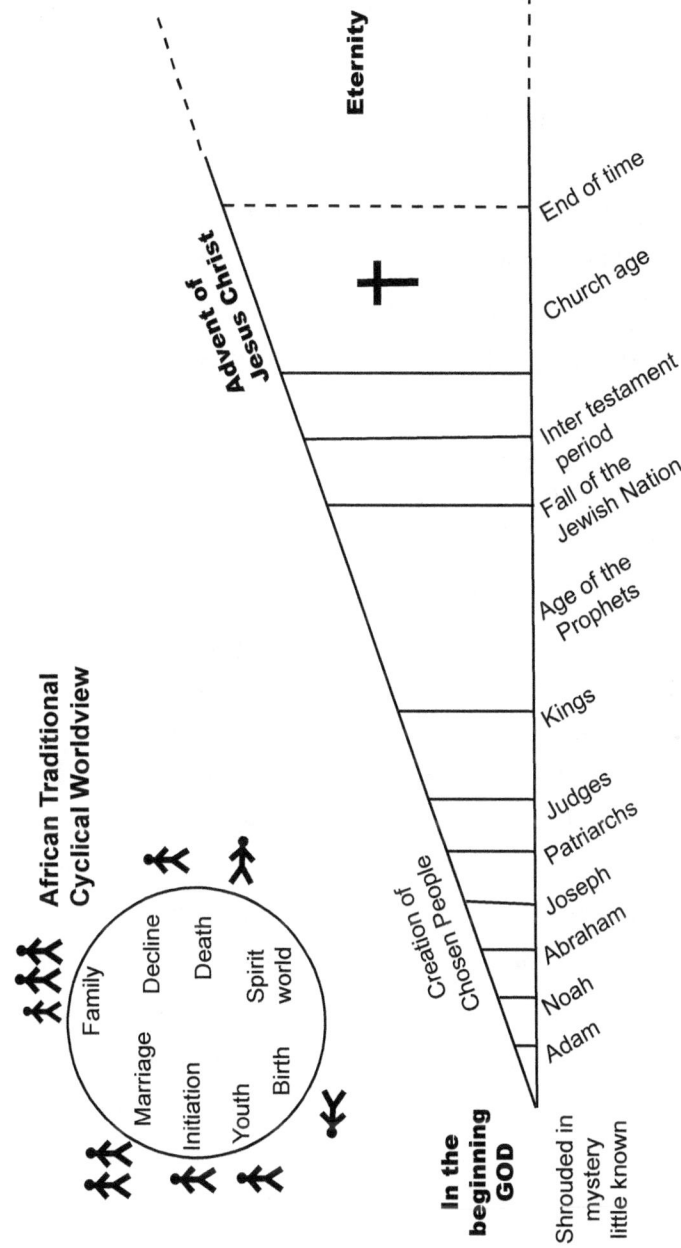

Figure 2 **God's Linear, Progressive Self-disclosure**

## Figure 2 **God's Linear, Progressive Self-disclosure**

It is a fascinating study to contemplate how God has revealed himself and his salvation in a linear and ever broadening landscape of his power, his glory, his love and his design to reestablish his reign over the cosmos. It is also interesting to note the Apostle Paul's claim as a prominent agent or apostle of that revelation.

A second point of great importance is that God's self-disclosure to mankind pertains almost exclusively to historical time. God reveals extremely little of the epoch which could be called "In the beginning God... ." Likewise, at the close of time we again see the clouds shrouding great mystery and the vast unknowns of how he is going to conclude time and even less about what eternity will be like.

Most of what God has revealed about himself pertains to his righteousness, holiness and love. Early on with Abraham, God made it known that he needed to have a special chosen people who would be a flesh and blood testimony to his holiness. It was through these chosen people, the Jews, that God would bring his ultimate self-disclosure in his Son who came as an ordinary Jewish boy who also was fully possessed by the Holy Spirit to the extent that he became the perfect example of God' righteousness in human flesh.

Through the divine Son, God destroyed the power of sin and Satan. Jesus Christ became the cornerstone of God's new creation, enabling people of all tribes and nations to become God's holy people. Because of his perfect human example, his teachings, his death and glorious resurrection, he became the first of many sons and daughters to be called and adopted into God's chosen people.

Romans 8:29-30 tells us, "For those whom he foreknew he also predestined to be conformed to the image of his Son, in order that he might be the firstborn among many brothers. And those whom he predestined he also called, and those whom he called he also justified, and those whom he justified he also glorified."

Thus, all scripture and any other revelation of God must be viewed through (and be consistent with) the example, the ethic and the teachings of Jesus Christ.

Finally, a word about end time events: There are hints and glimpses of what is in store especially in the books Daniel, Revelation and in Christ's teachings in the gospels. But these are frail word pictures of what all is in store as God brings closure to this age and ushers in his perfect reign and restoration of the cosmos. In Acts 1:8, just before his departure Jesus put some significant constraints on how much we are able to know about his return: "It is not for you to know times or seasons that the Father has fixed by his own authority. But you will receive power when the Holy Spirit has come upon you, and you will be my witnesses in Jerusalem and in all Judea and Samaria, and to the end of the earth."

Thus, faithful disciples will be consumed with being witnesses of God's salvation, holiness and love in the here and now. Several parables of Jesus call for faithful stewards in the absence of the master who will one day surely return and reward his workers according to how they engaged in his business until his return.

Figure 3 **The Apostle Paul's Cosmology**

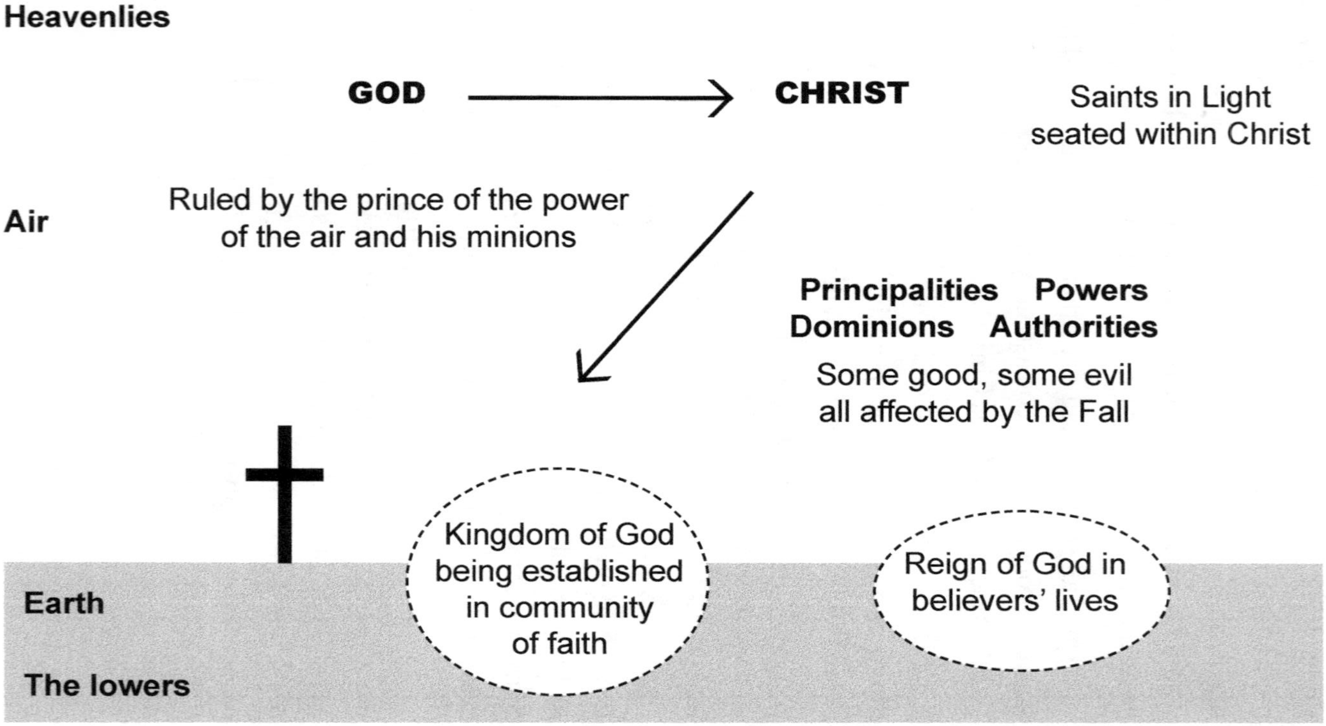

**Heavenlies**

**GOD** ⟶ **CHRIST**  Saints in Light seated within Christ

**Principalities Powers Dominions Authorities**
Some good, some evil all affected by the Fall

**Air**
Ruled by the prince of the power of the air and his minions

Reign of God in believers' lives

Kingdom of God being established in community of faith

✝

**Earth**

**The lowers**

## Figure 3 **The Apostle Paul's Cosmology**

Biblical cosmology is an attempt by writers of scripture to present an orderly schema of how God's creation is organized, where its various components are found and interactions between the components. The Apostle Paul's cosmology was drawn from his training in Hebrew scripture, yet it was also influenced by the Greek scholarship of his day.

Cosmology need not be an exact science and no one scheme is the right one. Cosmology helps us to know where God is, how he is intervening, the place of Christ and how he intervened on our behalf, and it helps us to know the locus of Satan, his demons, and the principalities, powers, the rulers of the present world both good and evil.

We will never know the absolute correct cosmology while we are shackled by the limitations of the human mind. We will not understand everything about God, what he is like, where he is and his complete nature until we are in glory with him and we have been completely recreated into his image so that he is able to reveal to us the immeasurable riches we have in Christ (Eph. 2:7).

I commend the cosmological scheme presented here as it is useful in helping us understand Paul's perspective and enables our understanding as the Spirit reveals to us the limited mysteries and glories of the eternal we are able to grasp with our frail human minds.

Figure 4 **Temptation; Short-cut to Glory**

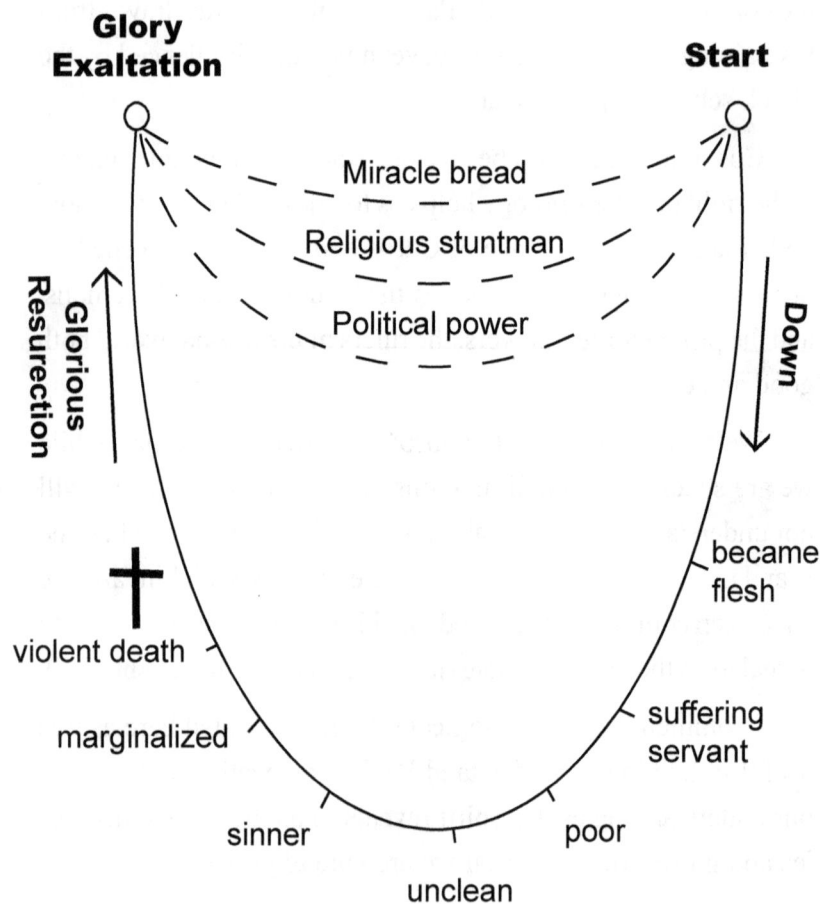

## Figure 4 **Temptation; Short-cut to Glory**

The story of Christ's temptation in the wilderness at the very beginning of his ministry contains an extremely important message for the radical community of faith. This story clearly sets out the parameters of how the church is to deal with the satanic powers we are surrounded with in our world as we occupy ourselves with the commission of bringing God's will to earth as it is being done in heaven.

Satan comes to Jesus aware of Jesus' destiny of future glory and exaltation, fully aware that victory will spell the defeat of Satan. To defuse Jesus' victory, Satan offers him some easy, short-cut tracks to Messianic victory. Satan continues to offer the same short-cuts to the church today.

God's way of dealing with the power of evil is to overcome and permanently defeat evil through redemptive love. Redemptive love requires the perfect one to become the suffering servant to the unlovely and rebellious, ultimately laying down his life as the means of reconciling the estranged one to God. This principle is spelled out through a beautiful hymn in Philippians 2: 4-11. The redemptive servant temporarily lays aside his glory and power to become a companion to the sinner, even to the extent of laying down his life. And in that sacrifice God is able to raise the perfect servant to a new life that defeats the power of the evil one.

To thwart that plan, Satan offers three short-cuts to exaltation, all of which avoid the humiliation, pain, suffering and death of the resurrection cycle.

The first temptation is to be a miracle-working messiah, who is magically able to feed people by making bread out of stones.

Surely that will be the proof that will persuade people he is the authentic Messiah.

The second temptation is to cast the Messiah in the role of a religious stuntman: Jump down off the temple, the very center of the religiosity, and safely land at the very epicenter of Jewish worship and cultic activity. Surely that will bring the Messianic acclaim he desires without the messy suffering and death.

The third temptation offers the short-cut of seizing political power to bring about an enforced reign of God. Just seize world-wide political power. Again, Jesus says no to this third option.

He is set on being the faithful Messiah who will bring victory through sacrificial, life-giving redemptive love.

The first two temptations are particularly prominent on the West African church scene: Be a miracle worker and a charismatic religious entertainer. The third temptation (bring about God's kingdom by seizing political power) is ravaging the church in the U.S. No end of Christian politicians campaign for votes to enforce God's kingdom through brute political power. The effort has made a laughingstock of the church because the Christian politicians are just as corrupted by power as their unbelieving opponents.

Let it be learned that there are no quick fixes to mankind's alienation from God. God's kingdom is advanced in our evil world only through Christ's sacrificial model. True disciples of Christ are actively laying down their lives as servants and facilitators to reconcile men and women to God.

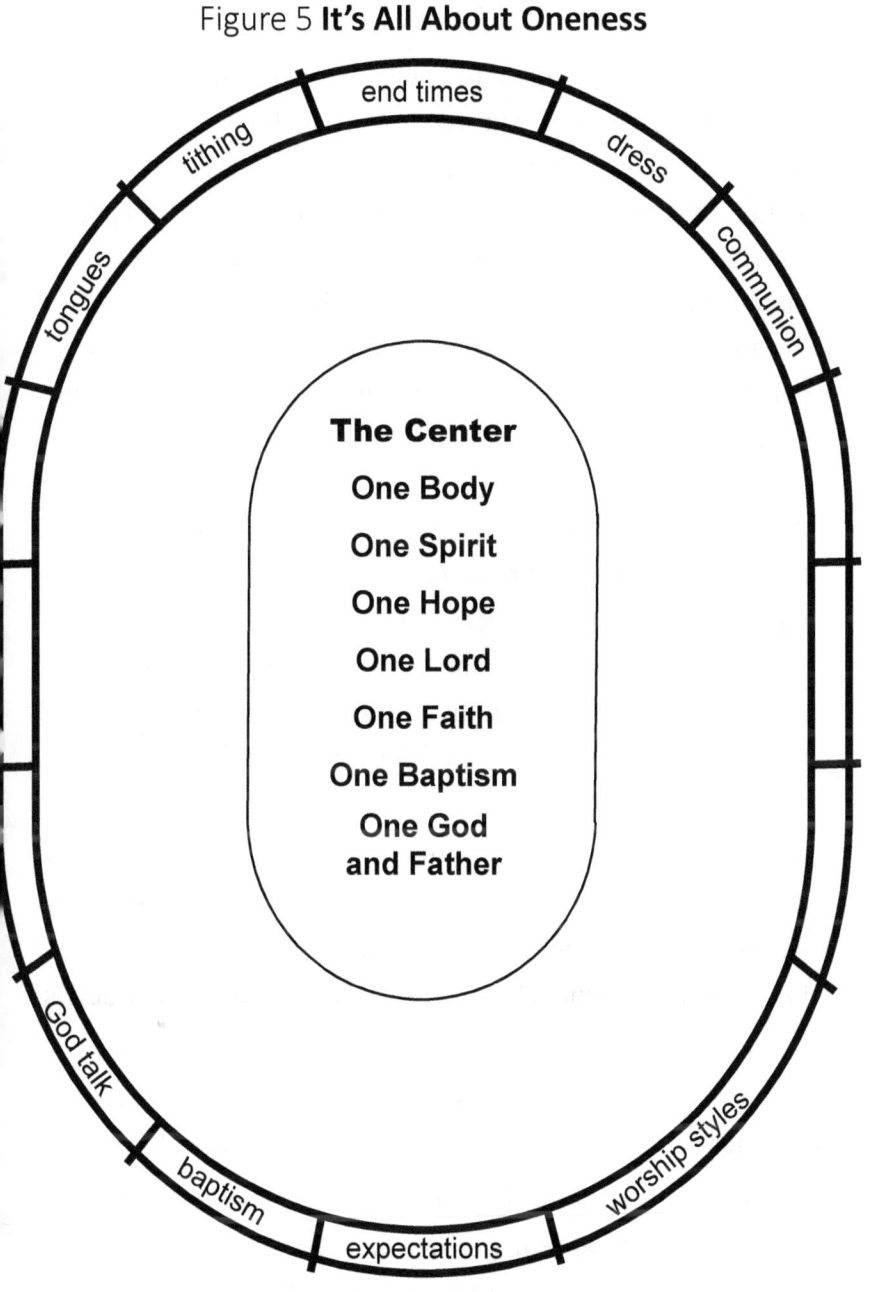

Figure 5 **It's All About Oneness**

**Let's Focus on the Center, Not the Fences**

## Figure 5 **It's All About Oneness**

An Ephesians highpoint comes in 4:1-6 where the apostle directs our attention to our true center: the body's oneness with God in Christ. It makes the reader wonder if Paul had access to John 17 where the Apostle John allows us to listen in on a prayer/conversation between Jesus and his Father. In a brief review of his ministry, Jesus states forthrightly that he has been faithful in carrying out the task God sent him to do. He was able to accomplish all that God expected of him because he and the Father are one; there is no variation of division, only perfect synchronization, and unity of purpose. He maintained the oneness even though he walked the earth in human flesh. Moreover, he pulled together a group of intimate followers who were now walking together in the same perfect unity with the Father and the Son. Not only that, Jesus prayed for us, many generations later that we too would share oneness as those who have believed and obeyed the invitation to oneness through the witness of faithful disciples who came before us.

Paul tells us our oneness with Christ and the Father enables us to walk (our behavior and comportment) in a manner that brings worth and worship to our Father. The way we live brings honor to God's righteousness because his law is written on our hearts.

Then Paul adds a list of virtues necessary for the preservation of our oneness: that our lives abound with humility, gentleness, patience and willingness to bear with one another in love.

With this oneness with God and Christ, enabled by the requisite virtues at the center of our faith and focus, we will have no-fail unity. Unity is lost when the church focuses instead on the boundaries rather than the center. We become guided by the fences rather than the center.

The fences are markers thought to bring uniformity, but they actually end up causing divisions. Fences are issues like tongues, tithing, end-time schemes, dress regulations, God talk, stipulations on sexual morality, modes of baptism, who gets to take communion, worship styles and many more. Churches that make these into litmus tests engage in sectarian battles with other churches rather than doing battle with the evil principalities and powers engulfing our existence.

All of these issues are dealt with in the Bible and I am not saying we should neglect them. The problem comes when we exchange our oneness with God and Christ (oneness of body, spirit, hope, faith and baptism) for the fences that just are naturally there when seeking God's kingdom and righteousness is at the core of our very being.

When the core is there, our hearts and conscience will not allow us to dress in a way that flaunts our sexuality; we will not give just a tithe but we will give it all; we will be faithful to our spouse or remain chaste if we are single; we will not speak evil of others and we will not be bent on laying up treasure on earth. The fences are implicitly there when we are faithfully focused on oneness with God in Christ. When our focus is at the center, God's righteous expectations are just naturally written on our hearts.

If I or another brother or sister needs help in any of these issues, the body is there, ready to minister and bear each other up with gentleness and love, knowing that each and every one of us daily live by divine grace.

## Appendix D

# The Book of Ephesians
### English Standard Version (ESV)

### Greeting

**1** ¹ Paul, an apostle of Christ Jesus by the will of God,

To the saints who are in Ephesus, and are faithful in Christ Jesus:

² Grace to you and peace from God our Father and the Lord Jesus Christ.

### Spiritual Blessings in Christ

³ Blessed be the God and Father of our Lord Jesus Christ, who has blessed us in Christ with every spiritual blessing in the heavenly places, ⁴ even as he chose us in him before the foundation of the world, that we should be holy and blameless before him. In love ⁵ he predestined us for adoption as sons through Jesus Christ, according to the purpose of his will, ⁶ to the praise of his glorious grace, with which he has blessed us in the Beloved. ⁷ In him we have redemption through his blood, the forgiveness of our trespasses, according to the riches of his grace, ⁸ which he lavished upon us, in all wisdom and insight ⁹ making known to us the mystery of his will, according to his purpose, which he set forth in Christ ¹⁰ as a plan for the fullness of time, to unite all things in him, things in heaven and things on earth.

¹¹ In him we have obtained an inheritance, having been predestined according to the purpose of him who works all things

according to the counsel of his will, [12] so that we who were the first to hope in Christ might be to the praise of his glory. [13] In him you also, when you heard the word of truth, the gospel of your salvation, and believed in him, were sealed with the promised Holy Spirit, [14] who is the guarantee of our inheritance until we acquire possession of it, to the praise of his glory.

## Thanksgiving and Prayer

[15] For this reason, because I have heard of your faith in the Lord Jesus and your love toward all the saints, [16] I do not cease to give thanks for you, remembering you in my prayers, [17] that the God of our Lord Jesus Christ, the Father of glory, may give you the Spirit of wisdom and of revelation in the knowledge of him, [18] having the eyes of your hearts enlightened, that you may know what is the hope to which he has called you, what are the riches of his glorious inheritance in the saints, [19] and what is the immeasurable greatness of his power toward us who believe, according to the working of his great might [20] that he worked in Christ when he raised him from the dead and seated him at his right hand in the heavenly places, [21] far above all rule and authority and power and dominion, and above every name that is named, not only in this age but also in the one to come. [22] And he put all things under his feet and gave him as head over all things to the church, [23] which is his body, the fullness of him who fills all in all.

## By Grace Through Faith

2 [1] And you were dead in the trespasses and sins [2] in which you once walked, following the course of this world, following the prince of the power of the air, the spirit that is now at work

in the sons of disobedience— ³ among whom we all once lived in the passions of our flesh, carrying out the desires of the body and the mind, and were by nature children of wrath, like the rest of mankind. ⁴ But God, being rich in mercy, because of the great love with which he loved us, ⁵ even when we were dead in our trespasses, made us alive together with Christ—by grace you have been saved— ⁶ and raised us up with him and seated us with him in the heavenly places in Christ Jesus, ⁷ so that in the coming ages he might show the immeasurable riches of his grace in kindness toward us in Christ Jesus. ⁸ For by grace you have been saved through faith. And this is not your own doing; it is the gift of God, ⁹ not a result of works, so that no one may boast. ¹⁰ For we are his workmanship, created in Christ Jesus for good works, which God prepared beforehand, that we should walk in them.

**One in Christ**

¹¹ Therefore remember that at one time you Gentiles in the flesh, called "the uncircumcision" by what is called the circumcision, which is made in the flesh by hands— ¹² remember that you were at that time separated from Christ, alienated from the commonwealth of Israel and strangers to the covenants of promise, having no hope and without God in the world. ¹³ But now in Christ Jesus you who once were far off have been brought near by the blood of Christ. ¹⁴ For he himself is our peace, who has made us both one and has broken down in his flesh the dividing wall of hostility ¹⁵ by abolishing the law of commandments expressed in ordinances, that he might create in himself one new man in place of the two, so making peace, ¹⁶ and might reconcile us both to God in one body through the cross, thereby killing the hostility.

[17] And he came and preached peace to you who were far off and peace to those who were near. [18] For through him we both have access in one Spirit to the Father. [19] So then you are no longer strangers and aliens, but you are fellow citizens with the saints and members of the household of God, [20] built on the foundation of the apostles and prophets, Christ Jesus himself being the cornerstone, [21] in whom the whole structure, being joined together, grows into a holy temple in the Lord. [22] In him you also are being built together into a dwelling place for God by the Spirit.

## The Mystery of the Gospel Revealed

3 [1] For this reason I, Paul, a prisoner for Christ Jesus on behalf of you Gentiles— [2] assuming that you have heard of the stewardship of God's grace that was given to me for you, [3] how the mystery was made known to me by revelation, as I have written briefly. [4] When you read this, you can perceive my insight into the mystery of Christ, [5] which was not made known to the sons of men in other generations as it has now been revealed to his holy apostles and prophets by the Spirit. [6] This mystery is that the Gentiles are fellow heirs, members of the same body, and partakers of the promise in Christ Jesus through the gospel.

[7] Of this gospel I was made a minister according to the gift of God's grace, which was given me by the working of his power. [8] To me, though I am the very least of all the saints, this grace was given, to preach to the Gentiles the unsearchable riches of Christ, [9] and to bring to light for everyone what is the plan of the mystery hidden for ages in God who created all things, [10] so that through the church the manifold wisdom of God might now be made known to the rulers and authorities in the heavenly places.

¹¹ This was according to the eternal purpose that he has realized in Christ Jesus our Lord, ¹² in whom we have boldness and access with confidence through our faith in him. ¹³ So I ask you not to lose heart over what I am suffering for you, which is your glory.

**Prayer for Spiritual Strength**

¹⁴ For this reason I bow my knees before the Father, ¹⁵ from whom every family in heaven and on earth is named, ¹⁶ that according to the riches of his glory he may grant you to be strengthened with power through his Spirit in your inner being, ¹⁷ so that Christ may dwell in your hearts through faith—that you, being rooted and grounded in love, ¹⁸ may have strength to comprehend with all the saints what is the breadth and length and height and depth, ¹⁹ and to know the love of Christ that surpasses knowledge, that you may be filled with all the fullness of God.

²⁰ Now to him who is able to do far more abundantly than all that we ask or think, according to the power at work within us, ²¹ to him be glory in the church and in Christ Jesus throughout all generations, forever and ever. Amen.

**Unity in the Body of Christ**

4 ¹I therefore, a prisoner for the Lord, urge you to walk in a manner worthy of the calling to which you have been called, ² with all humility and gentleness, with patience, bearing with one another in love, ³ eager to maintain the unity of the Spirit in the bond of peace. ⁴ There is one body and one Spirit—just as you were called to the one hope that belongs to your call— ⁵ one Lord, one faith, one baptism, ⁶ one God and Father of all, who is over all and through all and in all. ⁷ But grace was given to each one

of us according to the measure of Christ's gift. ⁸ Therefore it says,

"When he ascended on high he led a host of captives,
and he gave gifts to men."

⁹ (In saying, "He ascended," what does it mean but that he had also descended into the lower regions, the earth? ¹⁰ He who descended is the one who also ascended far above all the heavens, that he might fill all things.) ¹¹ And he gave the apostles, the prophets, the evangelists, the shepherds and teachers, ¹² to equip the saints for the work of ministry, for building up the body of Christ, ¹³ until we all attain to the unity of the faith and of the knowledge of the Son of God, to mature manhood, to the measure of the stature of the fullness of Christ, ¹⁴ so that we may no longer be children, tossed to and fro by the waves and carried about by every wind of doctrine, by human cunning, by craftiness in deceitful schemes. ¹⁵ Rather, speaking the truth in love, we are to grow up in every way into him who is the head, into Christ, ¹⁶ from whom the whole body, joined and held together by every joint with which it is equipped, when each part is working properly, makes the body grow so that it builds itself up in love.

**The New Life**

¹⁷ Now this I say and testify in the Lord, that you must no longer walk as the Gentiles do, in the futility of their minds. ¹⁸ They are darkened in their understanding, alienated from the life of God because of the ignorance that is in them, due to their hardness of heart. ¹⁹ They have become callous and have given themselves up to sensuality, greedy to practice every kind of impurity. ²⁰ But that is not the way you learned Christ!— ²¹ assuming that you have heard about him and were taught in him,

as the truth is in Jesus, ²² to put off your old self, which belongs to your former manner of life and is corrupt through deceitful desires, ²³ and to be renewed in the spirit of your minds, 24 and to put on the new self, created after the likeness of God in true righteousness and holiness.

²⁵ Therefore, having put away falsehood, let each one of you speak the truth with his neighbor, for we are members one of another. ²⁶ Be angry and do not sin; do not let the sun go down on your anger, ²⁷ and give no opportunity to the devil. ²⁸ Let the thief no longer steal, but rather let him labor, doing honest work with his own hands, so that he may have something to share with anyone in need. ²⁹ Let no corrupting talk come out of your mouths, but only such as is good for building up, as fits the occasion, that it may give grace to those who hear. ³⁰ And do not grieve the Holy Spirit of God, by whom you were sealed for the day of redemption. ³¹ Let all bitterness and wrath and anger and clamor and slander be put away from you, along with all malice. ³² Be kind to one another, tenderhearted, forgiving one another, as God in Christ forgave you.

**Walk in Love**

5 ¹Therefore be imitators of God, as beloved children. ² And walk in love, as Christ loved us and gave himself up for us, a fragrant offering and sacrifice to God.

³ But sexual immorality and all impurity or covetousness must not even be named among you, as is proper among saints. ⁴ Let there be no filthiness nor foolish talk nor crude joking, which are out of place, but instead let there be thanksgiving. ⁵ For you may be sure of this, that everyone who is sexually immoral or impure,

or who is covetous (that is, an idolater), has no inheritance in the kingdom of Christ and God. ⁶ Let no one deceive you with empty words, for because of these things the wrath of God comes upon the sons of disobedience. ⁷ Therefore do not become partners with them; ⁸ for at one time you were darkness, but now you are light in the Lord. Walk as children of light ⁹ (for the fruit of light is found in all that is good and right and true), ¹⁰ and try to discern what is pleasing to the Lord. ¹¹ Take no part in the unfruitful works of darkness, but instead expose them. ¹² For it is shameful even to speak of the things that they do in secret. ¹³ But when anything is exposed by the light, it becomes visible, ¹⁴ for anything that becomes visible is light. Therefore it says,

> "Awake, O sleeper,
> and arise from the dead,
> and Christ will shine on you."

¹⁵ Look carefully then how you walk, not as unwise but as wise, ¹⁶ making the best use of the time, because the days are evil. ¹⁷ Therefore do not be foolish, but understand what the will of the Lord is. ¹⁸ And do not get drunk with wine, for that is debauchery, but be filled with the Spirit, ¹⁹ addressing one another in psalms and hymns and spiritual songs, singing and making melody to the Lord with your heart, ²⁰ giving thanks always and for everything to God the Father in the name of our Lord Jesus Christ, ²¹ submitting to one another out of reverence for Christ.

**Wives and Husbands**

²² Wives, submit to your own husbands, as to the Lord. ²³ For the husband is the head of the wife even as Christ is the head of

the church, his body, and is himself its Savior. ²⁴ Now as the church submits to Christ, so also wives should submit in everything to their husbands.

²⁵ Husbands, love your wives, as Christ loved the church and gave himself up for her, ²⁶ that he might sanctify her, having cleansed her by the washing of water with the word, ²⁷ so that he might present the church to himself in splendor, without spot or wrinkle or any such thing, that she might be holy and without blemish. ²⁸ In the same way husbands should love their wives as their own bodies. He who loves his wife loves himself. ²⁹ For no one ever hated his own flesh, but nourishes and cherishes it, just as Christ does the church, ³⁰ because we are members of his body. ³¹ "Therefore a man shall leave his father and mother and hold fast to his wife, and the two shall become one flesh." ³² This mystery is profound, and I am saying that it refers to Christ and the church. ³³ However, let each one of you love his wife as himself, and let the wife see that she respects her husband.

## Children and Parents

**6** ¹Children, obey your parents in the Lord, for this is right. ² "Honor your father and mother" (this is the first commandment with a promise), ³ "that it may go well with you and that you may live long in the land." ⁴ Fathers, do not provoke your children to anger, but bring them up in the discipline and instruction of the Lord.

## Bondservants and Masters

⁵ Bondservants, obey your earthly masters with fear and trembling, with a sincere heart, as you would Christ, ⁶ not by the

way of eye-service, as people-pleasers, but as bondservants of Christ, doing the will of God from the heart, ⁷ rendering service with a good will as to the Lord and not to man, ⁸ knowing that whatever good anyone does, this he will receive back from the Lord, whether he is a bondservant or is free. ⁹ Masters, do the same to them, and stop your threatening, knowing that he who is both their Master and yours is in heaven, and that there is no partiality with him.

## The Whole Armor of God

¹⁰ Finally, be strong in the Lord and in the strength of his might. ¹¹ Put on the whole armor of God, that you may be able to stand against the schemes of the devil. ¹² For we do not wrestle against flesh and blood, but against the rulers, against the authorities, against the cosmic powers over this present darkness, against the spiritual forces of evil in the heavenly places. ¹³ Therefore take up the whole armor of God, that you may be able to withstand in the evil day, and having done all, to stand firm. ¹⁴ Stand therefore, having fastened on the belt of truth, and having put on the breastplate of righteousness, ¹⁵ and, as shoes for your feet, having put on the readiness given by the gospel of peace. ¹⁶ In all circumstances take up the shield of faith, with which you can extinguish all the flaming darts of the evil one; ¹⁷ and take the helmet of salvation, and the sword of the Spirit, which is the word of God, ¹⁸ praying at all times in the Spirit, with all prayer and supplication. To that end keep alert with all perseverance, making supplication for all the saints, ¹⁹ and also for me, that words may be given to me in opening my mouth boldly to proclaim the mystery of the gospel,

²⁰ for which I am an ambassador in chains, that I may declare it boldly, as I ought to speak.

**Final Greetings**

²¹ So that you also may know how I am and what I am doing, Tychicus the beloved brother and faithful minister in the Lord will tell you everything. ²² I have sent him to you for this very purpose, that you may know how we are, and that he may encourage your hearts.

²³ Peace be to the brothers,and love with faith, from God the Father and the Lord Jesus Christ. ²⁴ Grace be with all who love our Lord Jesus Christ with love incorruptible.

# Notes

# Notes

## About Beryl Forrester

The author's spiritual heritage is with the Anabaptists, the radical reformers of the 16th Century. As a young man he served with Mennonite Central Committee in Morocco and following a North American career in librarianship and farming he returned to Africa in 2000 as a pioneer missionary. He serves under appointment with Eastern Mennonite Missions, Lancaster, Pennsylvania.

Now in his 75th year he is still preaching and teaching the transformational message of Jesus Christ in West Africa where he intends to remain until the Lord calls him to his heavenly home.

**Contact: berylforrester@gmail.com**

## For more copies of this book

Additional copies can be ordered online at Amazon.com.

An Amazon page displaying the book can be accessed either by the author's name or the title.

www.ingramcontent.com/pod-product-compliance
Lightning Source LLC
Chambersburg PA
CBHW061638040426
42446CB00010B/1476